The
Centrist Manifesto

By

Uchenna Nwankwo
Centrist Books

i

Published by

Centrist Books – An Imprint of Centrist Productions
Limited
Email: centristbooks@yahoo.com

ISBN: 9798590551217

ALSO BY UCHENNA NWANKWO

Strategy for Political Stability (1988)
Economic Agenda for Nigeria (1992)
Overcoming Our Poverty (1995)
Anatomy of Politics in Igboland (1999)
On National Reconciliation and Development (2002)
Way Forward for Ndigbo (2003)
Zik, Ndi-igbo and their Southern Neighbours (2013)
Shadows of Biafra (2018)
Pro-Biafra Movements, Ohanaeze & the Future of Nigeria (2018)
Rescuing Nigeria from Internal Colonisation (2020)

If at first the idea is not absurd, then there is no hope for it.
– Albert Einstein

&

Only he who attempts the absurd is capable of achieving
the impossible.
— *Miguel de Unamuno (Sept. 29, 1864 to Dec. 31, 1936)*

PREFACE

Arguably, the bi-polar world in which the forces of capitalism and those of communism were stacked against each other in a deadly contest that almost ruined earthly existence is on the wane. In the one and a half centuries since the publication of Karl Marx's *Communist Manifesto* events have developed in a manner that has imperceptibly narrowed the gulf between the capitalistic and communist ways of life. This though has not happened without a lot of sweat, tears and blood. It appears that the old quarrel as to whether the means of production and exchange should be in private or public hands has rightly given way to a theory or notion that what property should be publicly or privately owned should be a matter of pragmatic analysis of suitability, and must be a function of time and place. The dominant feeling today appears to be that it is not who *owns* property that matters but *how* property is *used*. Indeed, there has been a movement away from the extreme ends of the ideological spectrum, from the Far-Left and the Far-Right, and a convergence towards the Centre.

Laudable and refreshing as the above changes and tendencies may be, it has to be observed that the Centre itself has for too long remained a varied, vaguely defined and nebulous concept. This state of affair of course introduces its own strains and stress on the world order and the organisational formats and wellbeing of nations. Conversely, all references and talk about centrist governments, including the notions of centre-right and centre-left regimes and philosophy remain something which like loose talk is very much in the air. Indeed, the strains generated by the status quo leave people and nations uncertain and disoriented, without an adequate and valid conception of events going on around them and in fact their place in the scheme of things. The disorientation and uncertainty of course create a dangerous and potentially explosive feeling of alienation in both man and nation. The situation therefore calls for more reflection, study and definition of the centrist ideology.

In the same vein, it is also germane that in dealing with issues of insecurity and peaceful coexistence in the world; in attending to issues about environmental pollution, safety and cleanliness, and other problems of common nature that affect mankind everywhere, no nation should be by-passed or left behind. In other words, problems of international nature should be handled by all concerned. What concerns all must be tackled by all! Policies to be pursued at the international arena should be democratically determined or sanctioned by all nations. The present system of leaving such discussion to a select few in the UN Security Council leaves much to be desired, more so since the composition of that council constitutes a stumbling block, a drag on the resolution of many disputes, with the veto used most often to frustrate democratic processes and to achieve, foist or impose stalemate in the Council.

What we have now is like a situation in which old-order leaders of the capitalist, communist, socialist and fascist parties in a country were brought together and asked to chart the political direction of the nation. Nothing useful is likely to come out of such a set-up, as such leaders are most unlikely to agree on anything. In contrast, it would be better to have a system in which *leading* nations of the world strive to canvass support for their respective viewpoints from the other countries of the world and have these participate in decision-making through democratic elections or votes.

Such consultations, we believe, will help stabilise the global community and would help eliminate or subdue certain misconceptions, ensure healthy development and revolution in our living standards as well as consolidate the emerging centrist ideology and the attractions and lure of multiple power centres and diffused or dispersed power in the world, as compared to a bipolar world that had presented a recipe for unhealthy competition and antagonistic relationships worldwide.

Nigeria, from which we draw most of our examples in this work, or the Nigerian political party system, is grossly notorious for its lack of seriousness; for the subsisting inability or neglect of the parties to articulate any worthwhile and valid reasons, agenda or ideology for their emergence, operation and quest for power. At best they present or offer, as economist Charles Njoku has observed, a comprehensive scatter of analysis and prescriptions that is merely meretricious and not efficacious to development, co-habitation and wholesome coexistence. The Centrist Movement International (CMI) is determined to deviate completely from this norm and hereby articulate an agenda or ideology that informs its mission of rescuing Nigeria and indeed society at large from inept, irrelevant and futile strivings borne out of lack of vision. As is often stated, "my people perish for lack of vision".

The prospects for the emergence and sustenance of the virile and fair society is a function of the viability of the vision and ideology upon which the society is founded, built or run. The absence of or the non-application of such a viable vision in the running of the affairs of the Nigeria country-state as well as most other countries of the world has for too long left the country and the world in general tottering in every sense of the word. To make progress therefore we must leverage on saner ideas, vision and focus to get the country, nay, the world at large out of the woods. Accordingly, we present hereunder a concise and abridged vision or ideology whose application to the running of the Nigerian state and the world at large would, in our candid estimation, take the country and the world in general to the path of sustainable development, growth, greatness and stability. The highpoints of this centrist intervention shall be pursued through the following routes or channels: (a) Socio-Economic Format; and (b) Socio-Political Format.

UN   **1st January 2021**

TABLE OF CONTENTS

Also by Uchenna Nwankwo iii
Some Dictums on the Absurd iv
Preface v

PART I
GENERAL FORMAT

1. **The Vexed Question of Social Egalitarianism ..** 3

   - Communism 4
   - Fascism 25
   - Capitalism 35
   - Socialism 43
   - Overview 53
   - The Centrist Ideology 55

2. **The Egalitarian Society** 57

   - Social Goods 58
   - Essential Properties of Fair Distribution 64
   - Normal Distribution 67
   - Skewed Distribution 70
   - Significance of the Normal and Skewed
      Distribution Patterns 72

PART II
SOCIO-ECONOMIC FORMAT

3. **Examining Nigeria's Socio-Economic
Challenges** 77

   - Movement of Individualism & Enthronement
      of Anarchy 83

- Parlous Economy &Social Disintegration 92
- Weak and Visionless Political Leadership 95

4. Recipe for National Economic and Social Development **107**

- Summing Up 119
- Universality of the Problem 125
- Policy Prescription 131

5. Efficacy of the Recommendations **135**

- Impact of Financial Indiscipline at
  the Workplace 140
- Background to the Scheme 146

**PART III
SOCIO-POLITICAL FORMAT**

6. Elementary & Secondary Distribution of Political Power **157**

Elementary distribution of political power 157

- Monarchy 157
- Aristocracy 159
- Democracy 160

Secondary Distribution of Political Power............ 164

- Modes of Power Distribution Amongst
  (Ethnic) Groups in National Politics 165

7. **Tertiary Distribution of Political Power**............. **169**

- Power Sharing Within the Proposed New
  World Assembly or a New United Nations....... 175
- Voting Power/Seats for Countries in the
  Proposed World Legislature............................ 179

ALTERNATIVE B

- Gradation of the Three Factors/Indices in
  Legislative Representation & Tri-Cameral
  Legislature... 193
- Voting Power/Seats for Countries in each of
  the Three Houses of the Proposed World
  Assembly or the new United Nations................ 194
- The Uppermost Legislative House 194
- The Lower Legislative House 198
- What the Proposed World Assembly is Not! 202

BIBLIOGRAPHY 205

INDEX 215

PART I
GENERAL FORMAT

CHAPTER I

THE VEXED QUESTION OF SOCIAL EGALITARIANISM

One of the central issues that has given rise to the development of various ideologies in the recent history of mankind is the concept of egalitarianism. This concept seeks to define the conditions that ensure an equitable or fair distribution of social wealth amongst members of a society. It is portrayed as the guiding principle in all existing modes of socio-economic and political organisations.

Pervasive as the concept has been rendered in sociocultural and political analysis, it is ironical that no concept is as controversial. It neither has any universally accepted definition nor mode of measurement. Most interpretations of the concept are based on emotional or subjective traits; thus making objective discussion of the subject difficult. Even more disturbing is the fact that there is disagreement as to what should be truly construed as the social wealth or social goods for whose distribution men are apt to clamour for. One is therefore, faced with a threesome question, namely:

(a) What indeed are the social goods?

(b) What constitutes a fair distribution of these goods? and (c) How can the fair distribution be achieved in society today?

For a meaningful examination of the above questions, it is pertinent to look back at the ways mankind tried over the centuries to resolve the questions.

First, we shall give a quick review of the major ideological theories of yesteryears. Subsequently, we will examine their exploits and applicability to the realities of today.

COMMUNISM

Communism arose as a direct challenge of the prevailing economic and political order in the 19th century Europe. During this period, the plight of the working class was to say the least, horrible, while the nobility and owners of industrial plants and other means of production and exchange lived in immense affluence and leisure.

Karl Marx (1818 - 1883) is generally regarded as the father of this movement having written the treatise upon which the movement was founded. Marx was dissatisfied with the status quo; the existence of widely separated social classes and was irked that the worker was not getting adequate returns for his labour. He had noted the rise to power of the middle class starting from the Magna Carta[1] through Cromwell,[2] and above all, that the 18th century French revolution had automatically "transferred social dominance from the nobility and the clergy to the industrial and commercial middle-class; it had created the state as a typical organ of middle-class repression and exploitations; and its philosophy — the system of natural rights in politics and economics — the ideal justification and rationalization of the middle-class' right to exploit the worker".[3] Marx felt that these revolutions signalled the beginning of a process which would ultimately transfer economic power to the people, the masses or the lower classes.[4] In other words, he thought that just as political power had moved from the monarchs to the aristocrats and then down to the people, so

---

1. Magna Carte – In 1215, rebellious English nobles forced King John to sign a document – the Magna Carta. This brought about curtailment of the King's power and led to decline of absolute Monarchy.
2. Cromwell, Oliver – the 17th Century English General who led the resistance that defeated King Charles I of England, culminating in the establishment of the structure of individual liberties and eventually to democratic self-government in Britain.
3. George H. Sabine and Thomas L. Thorson, *A History of Political Theory*, Dryden Press, Hinsdale Illinois, 4th Edition, 1973. Pg. 683
4. Ibid. Page 452; 682—684.

would economic power move down the line until a state of classlessness appears. Thus he felt that just as some philosophy guided the realisation of the earlier political revolutions so would the people need a philosophy with which to pursue the realisation of the latter goal. He therefore set himself the task of producing this philosophy. The theory of Communism so produced is known as the 'Marxist theory'.

THE MARXIST THEORY:

The essential principles of the Marxist Theory as may be found in *The Communist Manifesto*[5] are as follows:

i) THE ECONOMIC INTERPRETATION OF HISTORY:

The mode of production in material life is the greatest determinant of the general character of the political, social and spiritual processes of life. The economic conditions of a society are deemed to constitute the real foundation upon which is erected the superstructure of culture, law and government, and to which other forms of social consciousness correspond.

Closely associated with the above are the notions of class war and the theory of surplus value. Marx was of the opinion that the establishment of private property divided society into two hostile economic classes: the capitalistic class and the proletariat. The interest of the capitalistic

5. Karl Marx & Friedrich Engels, *The Communist Manifesto*, Ed. by D. Ryazanoff, New York, Russell & Russell, 1963.

class which derives its income mainly from the ownership of property is antagonistic to that of the proletariat which derives its own income from labour-power.

To explain this antagonism, Karl Marx puts forward a theory of surplus value. The surplus value is deemed to arise because labour power produces values above the cost of tools, raw materials and the cost of its subsistence. According to the surplus value theory, the capitalistic class through its ownership and control of the means of production, appropriates the "surplus value".

ii) REVOLUTION AND THE DICTATORSHIP OF THE PROLETARIAT

Marx predicted that a social revolution was inevitable as long as capital or wealth continued to be concentrated in few hands – a condition assured by the Capitalist System. According to Marx, such a situation would necessitate a conscious organisation of Labour or the proletariat, which would culminate in an overthrow of the capitalist class. Marx did not expect the capitalist class – at least in most countries of the world – to give up their position without a struggle. Hence, he argued that a violent and concerted struggle was necessary to dislodge capitalism. To Marx, this rigorous process of overthrowing capitalism would of necessity entail a dictatorship of the proletariat.

The dictatorship was however meant to be transient – a temporary stage in the march towards socialism. Since the capitalist class would not want to give up power nor property voluntarily, the proletariat would have to confiscate all private property, organise labour and compel all to work for the state by way of consolidating and perpetuating the results of the revolution.

iii) **THE NEW SOCIETY:**

The dictatorship of the proletariat is supposed to be a means for the highest possible intensification of the state and the realisation of socialism. As such, once it brings about the required results, the need for its own further existence and use would disappear. The dictatorship and the state would wither away because there would not be any more private property to confiscate. At this point, Marx assumes, the new or emergent society could be organised on the principle of "from each according to his capacity, to each according to his needs": Each man was to contribute to the social wealth according to his capability and take from it according to his needs.

These fundamental principles of Communism have been criticised by men from all walks of life from different standpoints since the publication of *The Communist Manifesto* in 1848, and still remains a source of great controversy not only among intellectuals but also among different peoples of the world. Even now, therefore, taking a hard and critical look at the theory cannot be considered outmoded.

On the materialistic interpretation of history, one must not fail to acknowledge Marx's brilliance in pointing out such a latent but strong factor in interpreting mankind's history. It is to Marx's credit that today, economic conditions of any society are regarded as very important factors in accounting for or interpreting her life processes. Before Marx, economic conditions were hardly reckoned with in this regard.

Whether this factor is the most important one is, of course, quite a different and difficult question. That any of such other factors like religion, politics, great men, etc., may take the upper hand or have a more pronounced or far-reaching effect on societal structure than economics is not in doubt. Therefore, while rejecting the notion that under all conditions, economic forces or conditions play the most important part in societal processes, we must accept the fact that they constitute a very important factor which could under certain conditions become crucial.

Marx's prescription of violent social revolution as a means to overthrowing the existing order and establishing Socialism stemmed from his conviction that the rich class would not give up its position willingly. In his view, members of the rich class were blinded by the dominant and prevailing conservative philosophy and so took the status quo as natural and therefore justifiable. Perhaps, if he had attached less weight to economic determinism, he would have realised that a possible emergence of new ideas could have weakened the prevailing philosophy thereby paving the way for a change of attitude on the part of the propertied class. In which case, it could have become possible to persuade them to accept change peacefully.

In fact, the passage in 1832 of the Reform Act in England and the Jacksonian revolution in the United States about the same time, which brought about power-sharing between the middle class and the aristocrats underlined this possibility.[6] However, since Marx viewed the world mainly from economic perspective he gave those revolutions only a fleeting and grudging consideration.[7] Since his thesis was anchored on the notion that the superstructure of society is built upon its economic foundations, accepting the view that the political gains made by the middle class in these revolutions could lead, in the long run, to a significant redistribution of economic power in favour of the lower-classes, would have run counter to his

6. William Ebenstein and Edwin Fogelman, *Today's —Isms*, Prentice-Hall. Inc. Englewood Cliffs, New Jersey, 8th Edition, 1980. pages 7—9.
7. In 1872, Marx admitted at a public meeting in Amsterdam that workers can attain Socialist objectives by peaceful means in certain countries, namely: England, USA and "perhaps" Holland.

entire thesis and belief. In other words, this would have given an apparent leverage to political determinism over economic determinism; hence, Marx's stubborn insistence on violent revolution.

It is therefore clear that Marx was guilty of blindly clinging to a pessimistic view. Surely, a class war or violent revolution cannot be the only means of change, as indeed the Jacksonian revolution and the 1832 English Reform Act, before Marxism, had indicated. Peaceful electoral process must be seen as an equally possible way of eliminating Capitalism or any other system for that matter. Reference is made here to the victory of the Nazi Party in Germany (1933) which ushered in Fascism, and the now commonplace victories of 'Socialist' parties in many countries of the world.

Furthermore, if Marx had given cultural, political, religious and other factors of social change their due regards, he would not have prescribed a dictatorship of the proletariat for the transitional stage of the envisaged revolution. He, for instance, discounted the political factor so much so that he failed to give sufficient consideration to the mode of power distribution that would follow the revolution. His dictatorship of the proletariat without a clear-cut leadership is akin to throwing political power unto a motley crowd and to chance. His hope or prediction that the dictatorship would crumble as soon as the new revolution took root points to shallow thinking and naivety. Even the injunction that in the new society each man would contribute to the social wealth according to his capacity, is to say the least, ludicrous. Who was to define what? If Marx believed that each and every man was going to willingly and honestly abide by such injunction without some form of coercive prodding, then he must have been an ignorant dreamer and a blind optimist. Ignorant in the sense that he failed to take a cue from the life of the social insects and blind in the sense that he expected a sudden and far-reaching change in what we may, for want of better expression describe as human nature, namely; the acquisitive and competitive tendencies in man. As Appadorai rightly pointed out, "a social ideal which assumes such fundamental change in human nature and habit is by the nature of things incapable of realization".[8]

As it turned out, these oversights were to stymie or delay the implementation or application of the Marxist theory until revised by Lenin.[9]

MARXISM-LENINISM:

"Lenin's most important contribution to the theory of Communism is to be found in his pamphlet, 'What is to be done?'"[10] published in 1902. Lenin unlike Marx, was more practical in his approach to Communism. Whereas Marx assumed that the working class would spontaneously develop its class consciousness in the daily struggle for economic existence and that its leadership would come largely from its own ranks, Lenin felt that communist activity is to be carried on along two lines. First, workers are to form labour unions and if possible a communist party. And secondly, there are to be small groups of professional revolutionaries, patterned after the army and the police, highly select and entirely secret.[11] This organisation is to constantly guide and supervise, much like the soldiers in a beehive, other communist-led economic and political organisations in the march against capitalism.

8. A. Appadorai, *The substance of Politics*, New Delhi, Oxford University Press, 11th Edition, 1975. Page 120
9. Lenin, Vladimir 1, (1870 -1924) – Leader of the Communist (Bolshevik) revolution which overthrew the democratic government of Alexander Kerensky in Russia to establish the first communist state in 1917
10.   William Ebenstein & Edwin Fogelman, *Today's - Isms*, Op. cit., Page 24
11.   Ibid

Lenin's position, therefore, amounted to a reliance on a perpetual dictatorship of the party as against Marx's hope for a temporary dictatorship of the proletariat. He did not delude himself into believing that once capitalism is overthrown, socialism would be sustained by the goodwill of all concerned. With Lenin therefore, the Communist Theory developed to a point of sacrificing individual liberty for perpetual one-party dictatorship. Having got this far, communism became ripe for application and export. It is now part of history that the first communist revolution occurred in 1917 in Russia and did spread to many other countries of the world.

Lenin's philosophy and contribution is no doubt more radical and assuming than the position adopted by Marx himself. Whereas Marx was ambivalent about the place of political power or its effect on societal structure, Lenin assigned little relevance to it. In other words, he failed to perceive or make use of the possible and detrimental effects that concentration of political power could have on the individual or society at large. Had he sincerely addressed himself to this problem, it is doubtful whether he would have opted for the permanent Vanguard of Communism which he created.

It must, however, be mentioned that in 1904, Leon Trotsky – then an orthodox Marxist critical of Lenin – predicted that the dictatorship of the party would be replaced by the rule of the central committee, and eventually a single individual would take the place of the central committee. This, according to Trotsky, was an inevitable consequence of Leninist concepts and organisational practices. The Stalin era proved him right. The brutality of the Stalinist era and the wave of purges which later characterised most communist states have proved a liability both to the world and the spread of Communism itself. They also did cast doubts as to the efficacy of the revolutionary method whereby these communist governments came into power. As such, there arose a movement and belief amongst some communists that a peaceful electoral process is a better method of pursuing power. Since this movement was mainly based in Europe, it is often referred to as Euro-Communism.

EURO-COMMUNISM

The basic principle which differentiates Euro-Communism from Marxist-Leninism is that Euro-Communism pledged to use constitutional or democratic means in the pursuit of political power. European communists (comprising communists mainly from France, Italy and Spain) declared that "all the liberties which are the result of great bourgeois democratic revolutions[12] including the traditional rights of free speech, assembly and religion, would be incorporated into the communist ideology. The declaration also supported "democratic institutions fully representative of popular sovereignty".[13] It approved "a plurality of political parties including the right of opposition parties to existence and activity"[14] According to this declaration, the final arbiter is "the verdict of Universal Suffrage".

Those assertions were further strengthened in 1977 by Marchais, the French communist leader, when he explicitly repudiated the doctrine of the dictatorship of the proletariat. He disagreed with the Soviet Communist Party about socialist democracy, emphasising that the dictatorship of the proletariat "does not correspond to the realities of our policy[15] and that "the word 'dictatorship' does not correspond to the realities of our goals and theses".[16] He made it known that the French Communist Party wanted to rally the majority of the salaried workers as

12.-16. Ibid., pp. 104

well as the working class on their road to political power. Accordingly, the word 'Proletariat' has been dropped from the statutes of the French Communist Party. The idea of a 'Social Revolution' is, therefore, to the true Euro-Communist, no longer fashionable.

Furthermore, the Euro-Communists have abandoned their earlier insistence of socializing all forms of capital. To this end, they have declared that small and medium peasant property, handicrafts, and small and medium industrial and commercial enterprises will be assigned a specific role in the construction of socialism.[17] This implies that large-scale business and heavy industries would be nationalized by a Euro-Communist government. However, the idea of paying any form of compensation to owners of properties so nationalized is not accepted by the Euro-Communists.

The philosophical basis for this insistence on confiscation without compensation is unclear. Perhaps it comes from the doctrine of 'Surplus Value', which according to Marx is undeservedly appropriated by the owners of means of production and exchange. Perhaps also the Euro-Communists think that since "behind every great fortune there is a crime" *(Balzac),*[18] owners of large-scale properties and businesses should be treated like criminals. If it were so, then the situation is grave. Perhaps, they need be told that even the not-so-great fortunes cannot be totally absolved from crimes. In which case, the question may be asked: why must the rich be singled out for punishment? Such isolated attack on only a section of the propertied class could, to say the least, be likened to a situation where winners in a long-distance race (usually in the minority) are deprived of their trophies or medals, not so much because

17. Ibid. Pg., 106.
18. Balzac, Honoré de, Author of *Pere Goriot*, et al, cited by Mario Puzo in *Godfather*, Pan Books, New York, 1970.

they did not abide by the rules of the game or competition, but because they were considered to have run too fast.

Now, it is not that there is anything basically wrong about changing the rules in a certain game or competition, especially when the prevailing rules are no longer capable of serving the ideals for which they were originally intended. But it is rather unfair and indeed retrogressive to formulate new laws which seek to destroy the gains of yesterday. The new laws must allow the winners of earlier competitions to keep their medals or trophies while ensuring adherence of all to the new rules in future competitions. It is when the earlier winners are denied those medals or trophies won in earlier competitions as Euro-Communism demands, that bitterness, rancour and hatred which are essential ingredients for counter-reaction, violence and civil disorder are given vent. After all, the rich could claim self-righteously that they played the ball according to societally approved methods and happened to be winners.

Under such a condition, the Euro-Communist commitment to peaceful change may become illusory or unrealisable even when they are democratically elected into office. In other words, a partial attack on private business or capital could boomerang, thus impeding the setting up of a Euro-communist government in a peaceful atmosphere — which is the very nightmare the Euro-communists say they are trying to run away from. Surely, it is doubtful whether freedom, liberty and progress can be built on the type of foundation on which Euro-communism is working.

COMMUNISM IN PRACTICE

The exploits of Communism started with the Bolshevik revolution of 1917 in Russia. Right from that date and even as the civil war was still raging, the Communists passed many decrees that had far-reaching effects on the Soviet people. For instance, Alexander Solzhenitsyn[19] who was an insider, in his many works especially, *The Gulag Archipelago*, has revealed a lot of what life was like or what happened within the Soviet Union since the revolution.

Generally, the Communists introduced many policies that brought the citizens of that country at loggerheads with the new regime. This was heralded by Lenin's demand, at the end of 1917, of the "merciless suppression of attempts at anarchy on the part of drunkards, hooligans, counterrevolutionaries, and other persons".[20] This was to include not only class enemies but also "workers malingering at their work" as Lenin put it, and peasants who refused to surrender their food and crops to the Central Rationing Committee.[21] These people were promptly shot, arrested or imprisoned. Millions were killed and many languished in concentration camps. The trend continued well into the twenties when Stalin[22] increased the terror many folds in his determination to see his collectivization programme through. It is estimated that between 1937 and 1938, Stalin executed 40,000 people per month —over 1,000 a day— for two full years.[23]

Collectivization of Soviet agriculture started in 1928 after the death of Lenin. Lenin had deliberately delayed this stage of the Socialist programme because the ravages of World War I and the devastations caused by the civil war

19. Alexander Solzhenitsyn was a Soviet Nobel Laureate, author and dissident who served long prison sentences in the USSR and was later expelled from that country
20. Alexander Solzhenitsyn, *The Gulag Archipelago I*, 6th impression, 1979 page 27
21. Ibid Chapter 2
22. Stalin, Josif Vissarionovich (1879-1953) was Lenin's successor who was named General Secretary of the Soviet Communist Party in 1922. After Lenin's death in 1924 he eliminated his political rivals to become a dictator.
23. Alexander Solzhenitsyn, Op. Cit. page 438-439

(1917 — 1921) had made immediate social reform impracticable. Hence in his *New Economic Policy* of 1921, Lenin had allowed limited private ownership of means of production. That Policy was meant to sustain production in the farms, workshops and factories while the new leaders consolidated their position. But after seven years of its operation and the consequent improvement of the economy, Stalin felt that it was time to enforce collectivization on the peasants. It is also possible that the Communist rulers felt that since mechanization was necessary to increase agricultural production, large-scale collective farms would go well with their plans to mechanise agriculture. In any case, the continued existence of private farms was a negation of Communist goals and served, Stalin must have reasoned, as both a challenge and a direct political and psychological threat to the acceptance of coercive political direction from the centre.

It is now part of Soviet history that about seven million peasants lost their lives between 1928 and 1933 while resisting the process of collectivization of Soviet agriculture.[24] Many died as a result of the famine that came with collectivization, others perished in slave labour camps in Siberia and the Arctic to which they were sentenced, while many were shot on the spot for their opposition to the collectivization programme. Certainly, there was marked resistance to collectivization from the very peasants whom communism was seeking to protect. Drives to nationalise other forms of productive enterprise in the Soviet Union were also resisted leading to purges and suppression. Forced labour became the order of the day while the nation turned into a Police State.

---

24   Ebenstein & E. Fogelman, *Today's –Isms*, Op. Cit., Pg. 30.

With collectivization, bureaucratization rose in the country. The effect of food rationing and centralised system of distribution became intolerable. Long queues of shoppers became commonplace in all parts of the USSR, causing an unquantifiable loss of man-hours.

However, even with all these sacrifices, it soon became clear that total collectivization was not the answer. It was adversely affecting the economy as well as the liberties and morale of the people. Furthermore, it became apparent that even the well-equipped security forces could never win the battle against isolated and, sometimes, mass civil disobedience. Thus, after some time, the government was forced to relax some of the policies. For instance, members of collective farms were allowed to devote part of their time to small plots of land for private purposes and management. Under this arrangement, an individual was allowed to sell his own products on the open market. Interestingly, although these private farms constituted only about one to three per cent of all Soviet farmlands, they were said to have accounted for as much as one-half of available Soviet meat, potatoes, eggs and vegetables.[25] Similarly, the inherent problems of over-centralisation did force reforms in industry, management, and so on, in order to accommodate, even if in part, the demands of individuality.

These revisions notwithstanding, there were still complaints bordering on the apparent neglect of the service sector and such other areas of life and industry where large-scale organisation is apt to be unsuitable. These include the repair industry, housing, catering, tailoring, and certain areas of transportation. It was to prove that revisionism was going to become an integral part of the socialist programme.

25. (a) Ibid. p. 32
    (b) *Time Magazine*, November 22, 1982, p. 22

Developments within tge Communist world are full of such divergent and conflicting interests between the rulers and the ruled. And closely associated with these conflicts of interests is a long history of purges and suppression in all communist countries. These happenings go a long way to underline the inadequacy of the communist theory, which in turn has led many communist regimes to apply 'reforms' in an attempt to meet with the yearnings of their citizenry.

Mass action against communist rule was to become a recurrent feature in many communist countries especially in eastern Europe, where the actions of the Polish Solidarity Movement seemed the most dramatic. The first of such explosions occurred in East Germany in 1953 amid general feelings of hopelessness and disillusionment. Living conditions especially with regards to food, had steadily deteriorated under the East German communist management. The spark which finally ignited the smouldering resentment of the populace in this country was a government announcement in May 1953 that workers' wages would be cut further unless production rose by at least ten per cent. With this announcement, most workers came to the conclusion that a more direct action was necessary to get the ruling party to give them more consideration and voice in the scheme of things. As such, they quickly organised themselves and took to the streets in what was to be the first strike and direct challenge of the ruling communist masters. The demonstration was nationwide. In many towns and villages workers occupied police offices, released political prisoners and set government and communist party buildings on fire. While many policemen adopted the wait-and-see attitude, some even crossed over to the 'rebels'. The demonstrators demanded amongst other things free elections, free labour unions and an end to Soviet domination.

However, the government would not budge. But as it was losing grip on the control of the security forces, it had to seek external military aid. It took a direct Soviet military action to save the then East German Communist regime from collapse.

Three years later a similar revolt took place in Poland. The striking workers carried the old Polish Flag, occupied the communist party headquarters as well as the radio station and set some prison buildings on fire after freeing the prisoners. Again, the populace was suppressed but not with-out some key government concessions to the people. Collective farms were dissolved and private farming granted to the people. In industry, harsh control over workers were relaxed. Limited private enterprise in business and trade was permitted on a 'moderate' scale such as in the case of bakers, tailors, plumbers, repairmen, and skilled craftsmen in the building and tourist trades.

However, from the mid-sixties, the Polish government under Gomulka, gradually curtailed these concessions and in 1970, it announced steep increase in prices of some essential commodities. Again, demonstrating workers poured into the streets. It took a combined contingent of army and police forces to quell the strike with hundreds of casualties on both sides. Thus, it could be seen that even in a communist country a situation akin to Marx's class war could develop.

Such episode occurred in many other communist countries like Hungary and Czechoslovakia. Also the 1980s witnessed a very determined and protracted struggle between the peoples and workers of the Polish State on one hand and the ruling Communist Party on the other. It was described as the bluntest opposition to communist rule. And it culminated in the formation of a 'free trade' union (*Solidarity*), which demanded free elections and the outright abrogation of the one-party system, among others. The demonstrations of '*Solidarity*' were so intense that the party was forced to change its leader. And despite subsequent measures taken by the succeeding regime to stop the protestations of the Polish workers, 'Solidarity', still waxed strong. The Polish situation attracted world-wide attention.

That most peoples in communist ruled nations were dissatisfied with the communist dictatorship was not in doubt. The way and manner different peoples showed their resentment to the staggering abuses of their liberties which communist dictatorships in these countries brought about may have differed but their effects and presence were manifested in one way or another. Where the government approach to the problem was not the kind of purges and suppressions of 'counter-revolutionary' tendencies reminiscent of the Stalinist and/or Maoist era, it was the more sophisticated methods of Brezhnev's Russia or an enhanced revisionist approach of some the then contemporary communist leaders.

The Hungarian government, it would be remembered did set the pace in economic 'reforms' in the whole of communist Eastern Europe. Under their revisionist laws, private enterprises of up to 12 employees were allowed to exist and compete in the production and supply of consumer goods and services. Hungarian entrepreneurs were said to have been quick in seizing the new opportunity. Hence, private business rose rapidly.[26] In other words, capitalism gradually crept back into the national life of those communist nations. Even one-time Soviet leader, Yuri Andropov, now late, fell for this model, signalling that the USSR could be on the verge of adopting the said Hungarian model.[27]

Indeed, the above prediction came to pass when shortly afterwards the then Presidium of the Supreme Soviet approved of a new law scheduled to be operative as from May 1987. According to Lagos' Times International magazine of December 8, 1986, the new law gave individual Russian families the right to embark on 29 different types of small scale businesses including land-cultivation for crops rearing,

26. America's *Newsweek Magazine*. Feb. 14, 1983, Pages 29-30.
27. Ibid.

cloth-making, souvenirs production, car-repairs, taxi services, etc. In proposing the law, Karanzki, the then Labour Minister confessed that the State had realised that it was not producing enough consumer goods in quantity and quality. The Minister also agreed that many Soviet citizens had jobs outside official hours, and claimed that the "new law itself would simply help legalise such illegalities". Of course, Karanzki insisted, according to the report, that the shift "does not mean nor signify any intent to return to free wheeling and dealing in private enterprises in the Soviet Union".

Furthermore, there were indications then that the shifts in Soviet policy could also take on a political dimension. Shortly afterwards, according to Nigeria's *Newswatch magazine* of March 2, 1987, Soviet leader, Mikhail Gorbachev, "called for an adoption of a multi-candidacy for elections for regional party posts conducted via secret ballots...". His strategy of overcoming the intransigence of the bureaucracy was epitomised by his policy of 'glasnost' which called for openness, candour and publicity, and public debate of vital issues as well as government policies and plans. "We don't have an opposition. How can we monitor ourselves?" he asked. According to the report, Gorbachev "spelt out his far-reaching policies for the democratisation of the country".

Such tendency was not restricted to Europe or the USSR. Other communist regimes the world over were caught up by such changes or pressure to change. According to a report,[28] about the same time China announced a mammoth expansion of its fledgling private economy, opening 40% of the country's retail business to co-operatives and even individuals while greatly increasing the freedom of its 800 million peasants to sell

---

28. John Woodruff, 'China to expand private economy', Lagos, Daily Times, Feb. 2, 1983

what they raised in the open market. The new commercial policy was also billed to expand the country's toe-in-the-water experiments with selling big-ticket consumer goods on instalment plans, sending more travelling salesmen into the countryside and increasing the mark-up between wholesale and retail prices.

The communique further asserted that the new commercial policy was due to the recognition by the Chinese leadership "that the centralised socialist distribution system it inherited from Mao-Tse-Tung was hopelessly clogged and would never be able to deal with the new consumer-oriented production policies.

In the three years since China began to relax its agricultural policies, peasants began to develop real purchasing power in some areas, but an inefficient distribution network failed to get the merchandise to the villages even while factories put more emphasis on consumer goods. The State Council, China's cabinet, acknowledged the problem in June 1982 and demanded reform. And the October/November (1982) conference was an attempt to fashion a policy detailed enough to give local areas freedom to meet their own needs. It was said that much of the new policy did not amount to 'new ideas' but to the enlargement of ideas tested in the past few years.

Whatever the official results of these 'tests', China was gradually sliding or shifting into free market economy. For instance, it was reported by observers of the China scene that free markets and department stores were springing up alongside side-walks and in small buildings.[29] It became obvious that if those trends continued, then Chinese rulers could soon be raced with the type of capitalist problems which brought the communist revolution into being in the first place. It was already being reported that those experiments had reversed the trend that

29. Ibid.

had given the state a strong-hold on commerce, reducing the number of outlets by more than 80% between 1957 and 1978, eliminating private shops and squeezing hundreds of thousands of co-operative shops out of business even as the population grew by several hundred million.

The *China Daily Commentary* described the result of state control thus: "The most common complaints of the consumer are the bureaucratic airs and bad service in state run shops and restaurants where the attendants are guaranteed their jobs and pay irrespective of their performance of duty".[30]

Reforms or demands for reform in China were not limited to the economic front. The prospects of combining economic and political liberalization took the centre stage in China's intellectual debates and discussions. The question was whether China could free its economy without loosening the political system and allowing more democracy. Since December 1986, this issue according to America's *Time magazine* of January 26, 1987, "has been taken into the streets. Thousands of students around the country demonstrated for more political freedom, often burning Communist Party papers and denouncing party leaders". This then suggests that strong undercurrents for western-style political pluralism were already at work.

From the foregoing, it became clear that the communist experiment was gradually but steadily manifesting its glaring limitations and was, therefore, shifting away from its avowed goals, although the leadership was very reluctant to admit this. That reluctance underlined a strong aversion to a full return to a capitalistic system. Most of the leading communist theoreticians and politicians were in dilemma. It was obvious that communism was on its death bed. It is no wonder that most communist governments around the world collapsed shortly

30. Ibid

afterwards, leaving what might be called pseudo-communist regimes in places like Cuba, North Korea, etc. Even China has bid communism goodbye; its economic system is decidedly capitalist even though its political system might still be totalitarian or anti-democratic.

FASCISM

Fascism made its debut in the first quarter of the twentieth century when Benito Mussolini (1883-1944) came to power in Italy in 1922. Its appearance was occasioned by two major factors: the increasing degree of social and economic stagnation that had crept into the capitalist world, and the rejection on the part of fascist adherents of communist and socialist principles as worthwhile alternatives to the capitalist system. German Nazism, for instance, was predicated on the Wall Street crash of October 1929 and the social misery, unemployment, inflation, and so on that followed.[31] Also it is probable that the events in the USSR where communism was already having problems did not offer any encouragement for the adoption of the communist ideology as an alternative system or antidote to the problems that gripped the capitalist world. It became inevitable, therefore, that a different and new method of social organisation would evolve. It did, and became known as fascism.

THEORY OF FASCISM

Fascism may be regarded as the second major twentieth century revolutionary totalitarian revolt against the prevailing established ways of life. But unlike communism, it does not have a rigidly stated philosophy or manifesto. It aims at establishing a social system, different from capitalism, communism and socialism, that would bring the 'good' life about. Much of what is known about fascism is based on Mussolini's own essay, 'The Political and Social Doctrine of

31.. (a) Thomas L. Jarman, *The Rise and Fall of Nazi Germany*, London, The Cresset Press, 1955, Pp., 125-9
(b) *Time Magazine*, Feb. 1, 1982. Pp. 14-17.

Fascism'. The theory of fascism is, therefore, basically an Italian product, evolved to justify the fascist movement in that country at the time of Mussolini.

Essentially, fascism is the "totalitarian organisation of government and society by a single-party dictatorship, intensely nationalistic, racist, militarist, and imperialistic".[32] The creation of a State imbued with the authority to dominate all other forces within the country and at the same time maintain constant contact with the masses in all areas of life, is the central theme of fascism. Fascist opposition to democracy stems from the notion that the majority is not necessarily more reasonable than the minority and that the democratic notion of equality of men is incorrect. It claims that democracy gives to the masses the power to decide innumerable issues about which they cannot possibly have the knowledge required to exercise sound judgement. Hence, the masses are often led by unscrupulous demagogues who use the masses to cover and carry out their own designs.

Furthermore, fascists claim that a popularly elected government is not necessarily the ablest. As such, they adhere to the principle that authority should be exercised for the sake of the society, but should not necessarily be derived from her. In other words, "the specific sanction of government is its power while its reasonableness is its ultimate sanction".[33] To the fascist therefore, the surest way of installing and maintaining an ideal government is not through the ballot box, parliamentary eloquence, formulating constitutions or any other such machinery but by finding and installing the ablest man in the country to the presidency, then leaving him to conduct the affairs of the country without opposition.

32. Ebenstein & E. Fogelman, Op. cit. P.111.
33. Appadorai, A., Op. Cit. P.128

Again, fascism is opposed to individualism because it does not believe that the conduct of life should be left to the individual. It is deemed that since the interest of the individual could differ from those of the state, the state must preside over and control all forms of national activity – political, economic or moral. Leaving individuals to control such activities would amount to encouraging opposition to the state, a situation counter to the fundamental principle of fascism.

Fascist opposition to socialism also stems from her attitude to family ties. Family ties are considered beneficial to fascist practice and should therefore be encouraged. Since the institution of private property strengthens these ties it becomes inevitable that fascism would be opposed to socialism and her doctrine of public ownership of productive property. In place of collectivism, therefore, the fascist promotes the corporate economy – a form of command economy which places the interest of the state well above those of her citizenry. The aim of this mode of economic organisation is often the preparation of a war economy because aggressive imperialism is the cornerstone of fascist foreign policy.

Fascism tends to be anti-rationalist, sentimental and stressing the uncontrollable elements in man. Instead of being reflective and open-minded the fascist is fanatical and dogmatic. This leads fascism to have taboo issues like race md inequality.

Whereas democrats see politics as a means to resolving group interests and differences peacefully and if possible permanently, the fascist's view is that politics or resolutions are temporary pending when he is strong enough to assert his might. Thus, he regards conquests as the inevitable end of social conflicts. Therefore, where a democrat would normally talk of opponents, the fascist would talk of enemies, stressing bitterness and lasting hatred which should, in his view, be totally annihilated.

The major weakness of fascism is its stress on authority instead of freedom; totalitarianism instead of liberalism. Instead of seeing the state as a means to developing individual personalities, fascism regards the state as an end in itself. It opposes the fundamental principle of human existence which assigns to the individual the freedom to think for himself, express his views, plan his life and grow to his natural height without dictation from the state or any other quarter provided he, in turn, respects the rights of others to enjoy such freedom.

Furthermore, the fascist idea of picking the ablest man to lead is naïve. How, for instance, is the ablest man in a society to be identified and selected without using the democratic method? What are the yard-sticks for measuring this ability? Is fascism not relying on a subjective value as a basis for its own realization and survival?

Lastly, fascists tend to lose sight of the time-tested maxim that absolute power corrupt absolutely and that the interests of the leadership may not always coincide with those of the society.

DEVELOPMENT AND PRACTICE

From historical records fascism seems to have found favour in relatively wealthy and technologically advanced countries. This is probably due to the fact that a fascist state with her nationalistic and expansionist policies needs to be self-reliant in the production of vital materials necessary for the realisation of these policies. It must be able to produce her own food, arms and ammunition and must also possess powerful media for the 'education' of her citizenry. Industrial, sophisticated societies, unlike traditional ones, create social and psychological tensions which could confound the people to the point of believing that only an authoritarian approach to these problems can curb such tensions. In the words of Richard Nixon, "when people feel panic, tyranny can look attractive if it promises order".[34]

Again, a short post-democratic environment seems to be a good ground for fascist development. When the democratic way of life takes root on a society it is very unlikely that her citizens would tolerate any curtailment of their liberties; whereas the citizens of a society with a young unrooted democracy may be tempted to see authoritarianism as a means of achieving 'quick' political results during periods of chaos and disillusionment. In countries without any democratic experience, a dictatorship is more likely to result from authoritarianism rather than the type of mass support which characterises fascism.

Adverse socio-economic conditions or structures constitute another fertile ground for the development of fascism. Unlike communism which is poverty-induced, fascism develops in a society bedevilled by social tension, economic problems and political instability which are usually followed by labour unrest, general social discontent, and ultimately, mass unrest with a craving for change. Under such conditions, the privileged citizens almost invariably, feel threatened and unsafe, and therefore, readily accept any proposition that promises immediate relief. An authoritarian regime would be handy in the circumstance: it would silence the labour unions and ensure the survival of the state or society. Besides, fear and frustration which poor economic climate brings about can also undermine faith in the democratic process amongst people. Unemployment rates go up, leaving the unemployed with a feeling of hopelessness, lack of sense of belonging, social rejection and lack of identity. Under such conditions, fascism gives this category of people a feeling of acceptance and comradeship by finding them something to do.

34. Nixon, Richard, *The Real War*, London, Sidgwick and Jackson, 1980, p. 46

With this background, it should not be surprising that fascism cuts across all social groups and classes. While the wealthy industrialists find that fascism could provide a check on their teeming and often rebellious workers, the middle class could find job security in the same system. As for the lower class there would be at least the sense of belonging, of comradeship, and so on, to excite their feeling of loyalty and interest. And, of course, there would be those who would support fascism merely because of its nationalistic, racist and chauvinistic appeal. These might explain why fascist programmes tend to contain contradictory promises – in its attempts to satisfy all and sundry.

The military is also an important social group that is particularly susceptible to fascism. Professional soldiers tend to over-estimate the virtues of discipline and unity even in a well-established democracy. Where democracy is weak, this professional bias within the military becomes a political menace.[35] This is exemplified by the attitude of the military in both Germany and Italy during the fascist era in those countries. The military would in the face of fascism either openly demonstrate its support for the system or maintain an attitude of benevolent neutrality.

But it must also be pointed out that the military could and do play a very leading part in removing fascist regimes where their level of performance is unacceptable. Indeed, once fascism or any form of dictatorship is established, the army remains the last bulwark of decency and legality with the force to challenge the establishment.[36] This explains why fascist leaders always keep a sharp eye on the military.

35. W. Ebenstein & E. Fogelman, Op. cit. p. 114
36. Ibid. p. 115

Italy was the first country to practice fascism (1922), followed in Europe by Germany in 1933. In Asia, Japan joined the fascist club in 1930 while Argentina went fascist following the overthrow of a landed oligarchy in 1943. This fascist dictatorship was built up under the leadership of Peron. Fascism in Germany, Italy and Japan collapsed with the defeat of these countries in the Second World War while that of Franco's Spain fizzled out later. As for the Peronist regime in Argentina, a military coup brought it to an end in 1955.

Hitler's Germany provides a typical example of fascist rule in practice, and will be examined briefly in this chapter.

Life in the Third Reich as Hitler's Germany was labelled was certainly a unique and intriguing experience for those who witnessed it according to most historical accounts. It was marked by regimentation and curtailment of individual or civil liberties. The terror of the Gestapo and fear of the Concentration Camps were rife. Communists, socialists, liberals, pacifists and Jews were endangered. By June 1939, there was a great purge of members of these 'enemies of national socialism'. It was a warning of the things to come.

Mass enthusiasm and support were imbued by an unprecedented and rapid build-up of the country both militarily, economically and industrially. It is recorded that by the autumn of 1936 the problem of unemployment had been largely eliminated.[37] Almost everybody had a job and people were generally happy and cheerful even though they got that far by being practically cowed or reduced to slavish unthinking animals. This enthusiasm and support from the populace was

37. Shirer, William L., *The Rise and Fall of the Third Reich*, New York, Simon & Schuster, 1960

not only as a result of the rapidity of Germany's economic recovery; the harsh treatment being meted out to the Jewish race was also a contributory factor.

Racial laws which amounted to exclusion of the Jews from the German Community was heralded by the so-called Nuremberg laws of September 15, 1935. It deprived the Jews of German citizenship confining them to the status of 'subjects". Marriage and extra-marital relations between Jews and Aryans were prohibited, and the Jews were prevented from employing female Aryan servants under the age of thirty-five years. With time, some thirteen new decrees supplementing the Nuremberg laws were introduced outlawing the Jews completely.

Nazi terror against the Jews saw the complete exclusion of the Jews from societal life. The severity of measures against the Jews were to continue and by 1938 one could see signs like 'Jews strictly forbidden in this town' openly displayed in German towns. But that was only the beginning of the road that was to lead to the massacre of the Jews in Germany — an episode about which much has been written.

The Nazi regime in Germany also saw to the blatant curtailment and deprivation of the rights of individuals to freedom of worship and membership of religious groups. Steps were taken to dissolve the Catholic Youth League. Thousands of Catholic priests, nuns and leaders were arrested while the leader of the Catholic Action was murdered during the June 30, 1934 purge. What is more, scores of Catholic Publications were suppressed.

The story for the protestants is also a sorry one. By the time the regime matured, the church in Germany had been brutalised, disillusioned and cowed. About the end of 1937, Bishop Marahrens of Hanover was said to have been induced by the regime into declaring that, "The Nationalist Socialist Conception of life is the national and political teaching that determines and characterises German manhood. As such it is obligatory upon German Christians[38]. It was a complete humiliation! The National Reich Church of German was formed with the exclusive right and power to control all churches within Germany.

Such embarrassment was not limited to the Church. Other facets of German culture were affected. In fact, there was a *nazification* of the German culture. Books which did not help the Nazi cause were destroyed. It was decided that all creative artists in all spheres be gathered into a unified organization under the leadership of the Reich. The Reich was to determine the lines of progress in the mental and spiritual spheres and also lead and organize the professions. Consequently, seven sub-chambers were established under the Reich to guide and control every sphere of cultural life.

These were the fine arts, music, theatre, literature, the press, radio and films. Persons in these fields were obliged to join their respective chambers and obey the rules set down by that chamber as guiding principle in their various works. Failure to toe these lines meant outright ostracism. Indeed, "political reliability" of individuals was a condition for admittance.

This meant that those who were even lukewarm about National Socialism were deprived of membership and hence their means of livelihood. The music of Mendelssohn, for instance, was banned because he was a Jew. The inevitable consequence of that 'bottleneck' was a rapid, appalling decline of cultural standards of the people.

Furthermore, there was massive suppression of freedom in manufacturing, industry and trade as well as a dictatorial control of German science, public schools, institutions of higher learning and the youth organizations.

38. Ibid

The agricultural sector was not left out in this totalitarian control. In September 1933, a hereditary farm law was introduced as a move to increase farm production. All farms of up to 125 hectares were declared hereditary estates that could not be sold, divided, mortgaged or fore-closed for debts. Farmers were obliged to work their plots. Upon the death of a farmer, the estate was passed unto his eldest son or the nearest male relative who must work the estate providing food for his brothers and sisters until they came of age. Every aspect of the life of the farmer was strictly regulated by the Reich Food Estate: his convenience was not considered important. All that mattered was to 'feed the nation'. Only the Aryan Germans were exempted from this obligation. However, despite all Nazi efforts in the 'Battle of Production' only 83% self-sufficiency was achieved in agriculture.[39]

In sum, the Nazi regime was able to mobilize the people for the sake of building a militarily strong nation at the expense of the people's liberty and rights to self-determination. Hitler and his hench-men usurped the powers to make vital decisions for the people: a condition which led the German people into the Second World War, which they lost.

The story of the rise and fall of German fascism is similar to those of other fascist regimes in Italy and Japan which ended with the Second World War. And as already recounted, those of Spain and Argentina fizzled out in the post-World War II period. Today, the fascist philosophy itself seem outmoded or over-shadowed by other political ideologies. Although one hears of attempts by individuals to resuscitate the dying creed every now and then, little or no success has been recorded. The non-existence of any major fascist party in the politics of many nations of the World today underlines the fact that the fascist philosophy has come under serious disfavour.

39. Ibid.

CAPITALISM

This could well be referred to as the movement of individualism.

CLASSICAL CAPITALISM:

During the early period of man's recorded history when population was scant and resources abundant, each individual or family unit was able to produce almost all her material needs, obtaining very little materials service from neighbours. Even then, these requirements came in the form of exchange of goods and services among families in what is known as trade by barter, or outright gifts from one family to the other. At that period in man history, there was little or no specialization. Each individual was able to carry out a wide range of duties. Division of labour was not known and there was harmony between work and property. Also the type of occupation (if we could so refer to it) that a person held in this pre-capitalist era and the price he charged for his goods and services were pre-determined for him by custom and usage.

With growth in knowledge and techniques, as well as increase in population, the economy became less localized. The primitive method of barter or exchange became less effective necessitating a more pronounced market economy. Specialisation was introduced with each person supplying to the market part of the product of his labour and skill. The products were no longer designed exclusively for the producer's own household or that of his neighbour(s) but also for the market. The forces of supply and demand, instead of tradition and usage as in the pre-capitalist era, became the factors determining price. Consequently, competition became a very important aspect of classical capitalism. This competition was fuelled by the fact that virtually everybody or family was a producer of something and at least a little portion of everything thus making monopolistic conditions virtually impossible.

On the basis of the above, the prevalent view in the classical model was that there should be minimal interference of government with the economic life of the people. The government was meant to protect the individual from violence, fraud and external aggression. Such functions undertaken by the modern state like the provision of education, unemployment-insurance, the regulation of public health, and aid to agriculture and industry would have been considered improper.[40] The individual was expected to be independent of government as far as economic activities were concerned. Economic liberty was viewed primarily as the right of each individual to undertake private enterprise or earn his daily bread by marketing his labour-power without government interference.

The argument in support of the above was that individuals would, in the long run, discover and aim at their own interests better than a government could do for them.[41] On economic grounds, for instance, it was felt that an atmosphere of free competition was necessary because consumers seeking their own interests would create an effective demand for commodities and services while producers, seeking their own interests would meet this demand leading to a balance that would not allow for waste in the daily production of goods and services. It was also thought that competition between consumers and producers on one hand, and among producers on the other hand would keep prices at a reasonable level and ensure quality.

40. A. Appadorai, Op. cit., p. 97.
41. Ibid. p. 98.

From the biological standpoint, it was deemed that the fittest ought alone to survive. This was regarded as natural law. Since the health of the social and natural organism was supposed to depend on the observance of the law of specific function, everybody should perform that function for which he is intended by nature.[42]

Such was the psychological atmosphere which made private ownership of property or means of production and exchange the cornerstone of the capitalist system. This was complemented by the wage-system of remuneration for members of the labour-force and the democratic form of government in politics.

Laissez-faire, a term which means government abstention from interference with individual action, was popular in England between the middle of the eighteenth century and middle of the nineteenth century. This was due partly to the failure of mercantilism and partly to the industrial revolution. Mercantilism meant government control over industry, trade and commerce. But the adversity brought about by the loss of her American Colonies about 1780, couple with the introduction of mechanical power and factories made the protective measures of mercantilism unnecessary [43]. It was felt that leaders in industry could take advantage of the concept of laissez-faire to achieve increase in production.

As predicted, there was enormous expansion in trade and industry. But the social cost of this progress was later to outweigh the economic gains. The market economy was further developed as well as division of labour and specialisation. The advent of machines and industrialization brought craftsmanship into disfavour. People now had to work in factories as labourers remunerated by wages instead of profits obtained by producing

42 - 43. Ibid. p. 98.

and selling their own goods and services as before. As such, the number of producers or those who owned the means of production fell drastically.

This situation brought about the existence and use of monopolies, oligopolies and associations of dominant companies in particular businesses and industries in fixing prices of goods. The extent of free competition was drastically reduced. Besides, employers determined or fixed wages by using all forms of manipulations to force their wills. Monopolistic purchase of labour, for instance was rife. As a result, while the owners of the means of production and exchange prospered, the workers' plight deteriorated. Inadequate wages, long hours or work, insanitary arrangements and over-crowded factories and homes, etc., for the working class were in vogue. The modern form of capitalism had begun to take shape!

These anomalies led to a reaction against Laissez-faire. Critics pointed out that:

> Free-competition can lead to the best social advantage only where there is approximate equality of bargaining power"[44] between labour and capital.

As was with Laissez-faire, "free competition" was free only in name; the employers in the long-run got their terms accepted by the starving workers. For the worker, freedom to reject the terms offered amounted to little more than freedom to perish. The argument was (and, I bet, still is) that society should moralise competition. While some people opined that social and religious organisations could provide the much-needed cure to

---

44. Ibid. Pg.99.

ignorance and self-interest of individuals, others called for direct government interference in business and industry.[45].

It was these periods and conditions that gave rise to enhanced socialistic notions of economic organisation. Note also that the *Communist Manifesto* was published about this period – 1848. However, all these calls and efforts to stem the suffering and hardships of the working class did not prevent the emergence of modem capitalism.

MODERN CAPITALISM

The major difference between the pre-capitalist era and classical capitalism is that while there was a high degree of harmony between work and property in the former, the latter brought with it the existence of a working class and a capitalist class. In the modern period, this disharmony has further developed from absolute *Laissez-faire* to a point where management and financial control of business are separable from ownership. This, in essence, means further alienation of work and property. The corporation may now be located thousands of kilometres away from the owners or shareholders.

This contrasts with the early period of modern capitalism when the owner or owners of business took direct personal involvement, financial and moral, in the management of their business. Partnerships involved very few persons, all of whom were involved in the running of the firm. Today, however, a managerial class of paid professionals see to the day-to-day management of many corporate businesses, making all the important policies, and even fixing their own salaries with little or no restraints or guidance from some other body or group of individuals.

45. Ibid. Pg. 99 — 100

The development enhanced the degree to which individuals can achieve unlimited wealth and also the trend towards big-business. The trend towards "bigness" can be shown if we compare the assets of manufacturing corporations for 1948 and 1976 in the United States.

According to available statistics,[46] in 1948, the two hundred largest manufacturing corporations held 48 per cent of all assets of the manufacturing corporations, while in 1976, their assets went up to 60 per cent. Besides, the five hundred largest industrial corporations accounted for 80 per cent of total United State industrial sales, 75 per cent of all profits in industry and 75 per cent of employment in all industrial corporations for the year 1976.[47]

Concentration of capital is shown by the percentage of people holding the highest stock. About 60 per cent of all corporate stock is said to belong to individuals but fewer than 0.1 per cent of the citizens own twenty per cent of all the individually held stock. In some major non-industrial sectors of the economy, such as banking, life insurance and public utilities, concentration of ownership and control is even greater than in industry.

With these developments, the classical model of competition has practically disappeared, since many markets have to be dominated by a few firms who often collude with one another on major policy decisions. This also implies that the number of employers of labour is steadily falling to the disadvantage of the labour force. One result of this, is a tendency on the part of labour to organise strong unions with the sole purpose of fighting for better conditions for their services. The

46. William Ebenstein & Edwin Fogelman, Op. Cit., pg. 154.
47. Ibid

emergent strong labour unions are daily at loggerheads with the employers of labour leading to strikes, lockouts and all manner of antagonistic relationships between the two classes – the employer and the employed.

On the other hand, where tacit or direct collusion is not worked out among the companies on important policy decisions, sabotage and violence become part of the daily struggle for supremacy among them. In this way, some inventions, research findings, etc., that would have served mankind are destroyed or suppressed in order to protect individual commercial interests.

Furthermore, because competition is localised, directed and forced, there is an ever-increasing rate of inflation. Since employers are daily exploring ways of maximising profit at the expense of labour the result is unemployment. In recent times, unemployment rates of up to fourteen per cent have been reported in some Western capitalist nations.[48] The extent and number of people affected by such rates of unemployment in rich industrialized societies with their overflowing resources or Gross National Product (GNP), or the fact that they are unable to accommodate all in the scheme of things, is the real pity of the capitalist system.

The effect of unemployment and lopsided distribution of national wealth cannot be over-emphasised. Generally, all forms of anti-social activities, notably crime, result. Men become susceptible to all forms of influences which frustration, abject poverty, etc., bring about. Drug addiction, alcoholism, etc., have become commonplace. In America, for instance statistics show a steady upward trend in crime rates as if in direct proportion to the increasing rate of concentration of economic power.

Statistics from the American department of Justice published in the *Newsweek magazine* of January 17, 1983

48. *Newsweek Magazine*, Nov. 29, 1982, page 42

showed that whereas 8.6 murders for every 100,000 of the population were recorded in 1971, the figure shot-up to 10.2 in 1980. Robbery recorded 188 in 1971 for every 100,000 people but climbed to 243.5 in 1980. Cases of aggravated assault is said to have risen from 178.8 in 1971 for every 100,000 of the population to 290.6 in 1980. Thus, it appears that as capitalism progresses, internal insecurity among the citizenry also increases. Man is turned against man and violence and brutality become rampant.

That strong links exist between socio-economic conditions and crime rates cannot be disputed. It is a fact of contemporary psychology that human behaviour is governed by both innate and 'environmental' characteristics.[49] As such, it is not enough to stress only the importance of individual virtues – self-reliance, endurance, patience, etc., or responsibility to create conditions conducive for individual actions. Rather, one would like to be sure that we do not lose sight of the intricate and complimentary roles which societal forces do have on individual attitudes. Even the strongest of men do waver under the intensity of societal or group pressure irrespective of whether the group is wrong or right.

49. Miller, George A., *Psychology – The Science of Mental Life*, Pelican Books, USA, 1962, Chapter, 14.

SOCIALISM

The origin of socialism is difficult to determine. There are claims and counter-claims on the subject, but suffice it to say that socialism as a major political force or movement is the product of the industrial revolution which led to the glaring social and economic inequality perpetrated by modern industrial capitalism. Socialism preaches the collective organisation of the community in the interest of the mass of the people through common ownership and collective control of the means of production and exchange as a means of solving the problems of inequality and social injustice inherent in the capitalistic mode of production. The point must be made, though, that unlike communism which sought to achieve similar aims by a radical violent revolution, socialism believes in the efficacy of the democratic process and so uses same in pursuing its objectives. Besides, socialists agree to the payment of compensation for nationalized property.

At the early period of the socialist movement, adherents talked of total collective control of all the means of production and exchange. However, this view has been progressively modified in recent years to exclude certain categories of property. Instead of total nationalization, the predominant view amongst socialists has become that public ownership is to be built-up gradually and by instalment. If one phase works, the next phase would be pursued. The feeling is that there is need to prove pragmatically, through accomplishment, the usefulness and practicability of public ownership in particular industries and services before moving to other industries. This line of thinking presumes that there may not be need for complete nationalization or collectivization of all means of production and exchange. This shift is mainly due to experiences from countries that are presently at different stages of socialism.

It is on this last model that some socialist parties the world over have taken over power from conservatives in a number of countries and at different times in the past few decades. In Britain, for instance, the Labour Party, Britain's socialist party achieved electoral victories in 1945, 1950, 1964, 1966, 1974 and 1997. It has remained in opposition from 2010 to date. The socialists have also presided over state affairs in West Germany, France and a few other nations particularly in Europe.

Because socialists generally agree that, "in places where small property has survived as a technologically efficient unit, as in agriculture, the arts and some areas of retail trading, services and manufacturing,"[50] collective ownership is unnecessary, "they have enjoyed long tenure in predominantly agrarian countries like Denmark and New Zealand".[51] This is mainly because farmers are sympathetic to the socialist programme which uses cheap credits and other such policies designed to protect the small farmer from the threat of domination by banks, insurance companies, wholesalers, etc. However, in industrialized countries socialism has not been that successful. This is exemplified by the history, achievements and perhaps, the future of socialism in a country like Great Britain.

SOCIALISM IN BRITAIN

The growth and development of socialism as a protest against the capitalist system is carried out in Britain under the flag of the Labour Party. Founded in 1900, the Party did not attain maturity until just before the 1945 general elections in that country, when it pledged to nationalize specifically-listed industries and services if elected into office, giving reasons why nationalization was necessary in these areas.

50. W. Ebenstein and E. Fogelman, Op. Cit. p. 210
51. Ibid. p. 211

With respect to water, gas and light, telephone and telegraph and other utilities, the reason for nationalization was the existence of a natural monopoly. The coal industry was to be nationalized on the ground of poor performance and inefficiency. Inland transportation by rail, road and air was listed on the ground that there was wasteful competition amongst private operators and that such waste could be avoided by a co-ordinated scheme and efficient public management. The National Health Service was suggested so that the best possible health and medical facilities might be available to every person regardless of ability to pay. As for the Bank of England, its purpose was obvious and the need for government ownership of the bank clear. The nationalization of the iron and steel industry was proposed on the ground that it was vital to the nation. In view of the strategic importance of the industry, its management could not be left to private individuals.

With the help of the above programme the labour party won the 1945 elections, and went ahead to implement the programmes although the nationalisation of the iron and steel industry was left out.

There has been further socialisation since 1945. A social security scheme was set up with the aim of providing protection against sickness, unemployment and old age. There are also maternity grants, widows' pensions and family allowances. In the years beginning from 1945 to 1956 further policies of the Labour government aimed at greater social equality and the enhancement of the basic institutions of the welfare state including the provision of educational opportunities for all were introduced: new colleges and universities were founded in an attempt to provide education for many rather than the selected few. The Labour Party tackled the problem of segregation in the education of different classes of people. The tendency toward academic education for a small minority of high class children, which led to college and vocational education for the mass of the people, was curbed.

Taxation was also used as an effective instrument of reducing inequalities in income. Through progressive taxation, the net income of the upper class was drastically reduced. Estate or inheritance taxes were raised as high as 80 percent. The effects of these measures were significant. Whereas in 1911, the top one per cent of the British population held about 69 per cent of the nation's wealth, the share was reduced to about 25 per cent by 1980.[52] Similarly, the share for the top 10 per cent is reported to have fallen from 92 per cent in 1911 to 50 per cent of the nation's wealth. It is also reported that there has been a sharp increase in the size of the middle income group.[53] Also, the proportion of national income paid in wages and salaries increased from 60 per cent in 1938 to 70 per cent in about 1980.[54]

That the Labour party did achieve much in terms of social justice and egalitarianism in the British society is not in doubt. But much remains to be done – and this at a period when even the party seems to have come to the inevitable decision that further socialization and nationalisation is no longer the best way of tackling the problems of inequality. The philosophy of pragmatic nationalisation and socialisation has therefore lost its impulse as a force for social-economic upliftment. As such, the trend towards a more equitable distribution of national wealth has lost its steam and would hover around the level already recounted or might even slide backwards unless, of course, drastic steps are taken to further correct the imbalance.

52. Ibid. p. 232.
53. Ibid.
54. Ibid.

PROBLEMS OF NATIONALIZATION

Socialist theory and practice have undergone marked changes on the issue of nationalisation in the past few decades. Faced with realities, the earlier socialist orthodox principles came into disfavour shifting to the doctrine of "limited and pragmatic nationalization".

The shift in emphasis and adherence to the orthodox principles are due primarily to the problems which arose from such practice. The first to come to mind is the issue of big government. In the parlance of early liberalism, the best government is that which governs least, that is a government which interferes least with the economic life of the people. Nationalisation of means of production and exchange implies increased state control and regulation in the economic life of the people. It brings about concentration of power in the hands of the rulers. And since individual freedom is inextricably linked to the diffusion of power (political as well as economic), we find that individual and political liberties are steadily eroded or sacrificed at the altar of increased nationalization.

Secondly, the case against nationalization is strong in industries that demand high adaptability to changing conditions. These include industries that produce largely for export or that operate with considerable elements of risk and competition. Because bureaucratically run enterprises tend to put security above adventure, risks and experimentation, publicly-run businesses tend to be incompatible with rapid industrial expansion or the rapidly changing mode of industrial production that characterizes our age. As such, it has been argued that limited public ownership and control does not necessarily lead to increased production (especially with respect to quality) or general improvement of a national economy. Rather, most people argue that on the contrary, collective ownership weakens, at least in the long run, the national economy by artificially propping up declining industries which should have been allowed to die. In the attempt to protect these industries, especially their workers, the health of the national economy is often neglected by socialist government.

On the other hand, limited public control of the means of production hardly produces the much desired reduction in economic inequality. Experience in most developing countries where governments own many industries testify to this. In Nigeria, for instance, most public-owned enterprises depend on government's grants for their continued survival, while well-placed individuals within such organisations amass stupendous fortunes (millions of naira) within a short period of time.

Furthermore, in competitive enterprises, where flexibility and innovation are essential nationalized industries find it more difficult to attract top-quality executives. This is because, as an enterprise is nationalized, it becomes monopolistic and routinized allowing less creativity and executive initiative. Also nationalized enterprises are generally regulated to the point of paying lower executive salaries thereby driving away abler executives to non-publicly-owned enterprises.

Lastly, high degree of nationalization brings about all forms of socio-political problems. A small political crisis – the type that would normally go unnoticed in less socialized nations – tends to paralyse a whole national economy in predominantly socialist countries. In Portugal, for instance, where a petty feud in Parliament shattered the governing centre-right coalition in February 1983, the ripples were felt by nearly all facets of the national economy.[55] The minor crisis which erupted before Parliament could pass the 1983 budget paralysed the state enterprises which embraced close to 70% of the country's industries.

55. *Newsweek Magazine*, Feb. 21, 1983; *Time Magazine*, Feb 14, 1983.

They were left without funds and direction. The construction industry, said to be the country's biggest employer of labour, virtually collapsed because of lack of new jobs and materials.[56]

There is no gainsaying the fact that if these enterprises were not so centralised or nationalized, the entire nation would not have been subjected to such a high degree of economic paralysis. The 'political crisis would not have been much more than the politicians' headache!

Because of these complex problems, many leading socialists are increasingly reconciling themselves to virtually complete elimination of public ownership and control of means of production and exchange. But they still favour socialization in the service and welfare sectors of the economy. The general feeling is that governments are not efficient at producing goods but could play an effective role in the area redistribution of income and wealth.

PROBLEMS OF SOCIALIZATION AND WELFARE

Although the concept of socialization of services and welfare has enjoyed the most popular support and success of all socialist principles, it is not by any means devoid of defects. But the extent to which these defects are felt depend on what areas and to what degree the principle is applied within the society. Where welfare has concentrated on payment of unemployment benefits and the like instead of providing gainful employment to the unemployed, resentment against *welfarism* is pronounced. Generally, there seems to be a deep-seated psychological reaction against the dole. Normally, individuals regard living on the dole or welfare as more disgraceful than poverty itself. Hence, some people accept such reliefs only in moments of extreme deprivation, while some would rather steal than accept government hand-outs.

56. Ibid.

Furthermore, such reliefs have the potential of creating and encouraging the existence of a class of loafers – people who would rather parasite on society than exploit available opportunities to channel their energies into useful ventures. Lazy adults find such conditions conducive to their inclinations to waltz through life: drinking and making merry at the expense of the employed labour force or society in general.

Also, where welfare amounts to indiscriminate provision of elaborate child-care schemes, free education and free health care, the tendency is for people, loafers as well as usefully employed citizens, to breed children at will trusting that government would come to their rescue when it comes to the children's training and upbringing. The result of course is a high rate of national population growth.

Too much governmental involvement in the up-bringing of children may rob the parents of their primary responsibility to their offspring leading to a progressive weakening of the very fabrics of the family institution. And since the family is the microcosm of society, this also implies weakening the entire societal structure. As such, too much state interference results in indiscipline and juvenile delinquency because such usurpation of parental duties reduces the chances of parental control and guidance over children – an aspect of child education which the state can hardly imbue in children.

Furthermore, many who advocate for increased socialization of services on the grounds of reducing inequality of wealth distribution between individuals and classes within a society often lose sight of the fact that the very concept or application of socialization could equally bring about increased inequality between sub-national groups and therefore, in the long run, negate the very reasons for which it was applied. This assertion is particularly applicable in a heterogeneous society made up of sub-national groups that are at varying levels of development.

Because the disparity in development could give rise to a corresponding disparity in needs for certain services (or their socialization) amongst the various constituent groups, we find that socialization of given service might amount to society paying for a service that is enjoyed predominantly by only a group or segment of society. This could lead to a progressive exploitation of groups that have least need for that service since they are now forced to pay more (say, by way of taxation) than they normally would have paid for that service if it were not socialized.

A case in point is the socialization of education in a country where the different constituent groups or sections are not at the same level of educational advancement. By socialization here, we mean that the central government undertakes to pay the cost of education (at all levels) in the country. If that country consists of two sections that are equally populated but one section provides, say, eighty per cent of the pupils in the educational institutions while the other has only twenty per cent then the "free education" or full socialization of education would, in the final analysis, contribute towards a disproportionate distribution of societal wealth amongst the two segments of the society, unless, of course, there is another socialized service which is predominantly enjoyed by the disadvantaged group or section to the extent of offsetting the imbalance caused by the socialization of education.

These limitations are increasingly raising questions as to the soundness of continued government involvement or expansion of welfare programmes. While extremist opponents of welfare demand that the problems of poverty and unemployment be left to private and voluntary organisations, moderates opine that there should be limited government involvement designed to complement, not displace parental, family or other voluntary institutions.

The popular view is that avenues where government involvement produces the best social ends should be explored.   But many do not delude themselves that such socialization would solve the increasing rates of social stagnation that is afflicting many countries today, and that it is hardly applicable in developing countries where fund and resources are scant. Not even the rich countries are entirely comfortable with paying the bills of socialization. The strain in many European economies over welfare bills is a case in point.[57]

57. *Newsweek Magazine*, July 25, 1983, pp. 8 - 14

OVERVIEW

We have in the preceding sections examined four political ideologies that have evolved in contemporary human history and how their applications affect or are likely to affect societies. From those sections also we can easily discern that the distinctions among these ideologies are based on: -

    (a) whether the economy is predominantly in private hands or is publicly controlled; and

    (b) whether the political system is based on one party dictatorship or multi-party democracy.

Capitalism, for instance, combines private ownership with the multi-party system while Communism combines public ownership with one party system. Unlike socialism which combines public ownership with multi-party system, fascism combines private ownership with one-party system.

These distinctions raise questions as to whether fascism tends more towards capitalism (because the means of production are in private hands) or towards communism because of its adherence to one-party dictatorship). Or whether socialism is nearer to capitalism (because of its commitment to the multi-party democratic tradition), or communism (because it subscribes to public ownership and control of the means of production).

Such discussions underline the fact that capitalism and communism are the dominant ideologies not only because of their enormous influence the world over but also because of their philological standpoints. Hence, the ideological spectrum is often conceived as a linear one with capitalism and communism at the two extreme and opposing ends, while socialism and fascism fall at different points along this line.

Because of the relative weakness of socialism and fascism, capitalism and communism constituted the two major ideological forces, that kind of divided the world into two major opposing blocks. So strong was commitment and adherence of different peoples and nations the world over to these blocks that the future and survival of mankind appeared largely dependent on the lure of the relationship between the two erstwhile blocks. These differences gave rise to severe international tension and intrigues as well as civil disorder and confusion in many countries of the world. This is not to say that our world has now become so unified as to go without tensions!

However, it does appear that everybody, every group is beginning to come to the realisation that neither of the four political ideologies we have been looking at is perfect, and that there is need for a genuine and sober reflection and re-examination of our socioeconomic organisational formats as well as a deepening of our socio-political thought processes especially as it pertains to international relations.

In searching for a more relaxed international relation, therefore, one must not lose sight of this important root cause of the severe tensions of the past and today. And considering the defects already enumerated for each of the four existing ideologies, one cannot but opine that mankind has come to a point where a new set of ideas or organisational format is required for better governance of peoples the world over, the achievement of global stability, unity and wellbeing included.

Of course, such a set of ideas must be capable of universal acceptance if it is to deflate international tension and also be able to reconcile the authority of the state with the liberty of the individuals within nations. Common-sense dictates that such a body of ideas must be at once socialistic and individualistic as well as globally conscious and encompassing.

THE CENTRIST IDEOLOGY

Arguably, the bi-polar world in which the forces of capitalism and those of communism were stacked against each other in a deadly contest that almost ruined earthly existence is on the wane. In the one and a half centuries since the publication of Karl Marx's *Communist Manifesto* events have developed in a manner that has imperceptibly narrowed the gulf between the capitalistic and communist ways of life. This though has not happened without a lot of tears, sweat and blood.

However, it appears that the old quarrel as to whether the means of production and exchange should be in private or public hands has given way to a theory or notion that what property should be publicly or privately owned should be a matter of pragmatic analysis of suitability, and must be a function of time and place. The dominant feeling today appears to be that it is not *who owns property* that matters but *how property* is *used*. Indeed, there has been a movement away from the extreme ends of the ideological spectrum, from the Far-Left and the Far-Right, and a convergence towards the Centre.

Laudable and refreshing as the above changes and tendencies may be, it has to be observed that the Centre itself has for too long remained a varied, vaguely defined and nebulous concept. This state of affair of course introduces its own strains and stress on the world order and the organisational formats and wellbeing of nations. Conversely, all references and talk about centrist governments, including the notions of centre-right and centre-left regimes and philosophy remain something which like loose talk is very much in the air.

Indeed, the strains generated by the status quo leave people and nations uncertain and disoriented, without an adequate and valid conception of events going on around them and in fact their place in the scheme of things. The disorientation and uncertainty of course create a dangerous and potentially explosive feeling of alienation in both man and nation. The situation therefore calls for more reflection, study and definition of this centrist ideology.

Since the centrist ideology is one that aims at avoiding the drawbacks or mischievous aspects of the old political ideologies, of combining the best aspects of the socialistic and capitalistic ideologies to create a new wholesome idea or pattern, we need ab initio to delve into and in fact define the fundamental characteristics of the fair or egalitarian s   ociety and signpost the achievement of these as the goal of the centrist ideology. As a consequence, we shall in the next chapter turn attention to a concise study of the egalitarian society and its major defining characteristics – at least with respect to the distribution or the sharing of those most essential *goods* and their perquisites within a group or society that men are apt to clamour for.

CHAPTER 2

THE EGALITARIAN SOCIETY

Most of the squabbles and conflicts that pervade our planet today are traceable to the inability on the part of societies to work out appropriate methods of sharing jointly-owned resources and commonly-earned incomes. In industry, there is the age-old problem of relations of production, of distribution of income and the appropriation of what Karl Marx called "surplus value". This partly results in disagreements between capital and labour over what proportion of the 'value-added' or fruits of a venture is appropriated and by whom. Among sub-national groups as well as other primary and secondary groups the same problem is noticeable in revenue allocations and power-sharing processes. Even international relations are not spared of this problem. In fact, they appear to be the arena where the contest is hottest given the claim of every nation to sovereignty and the freedom to act as it deems fit.

Over the centuries, lasting and permanent solutions to the above problems have been elusive for a number of reasons, one of which is the absence of a generally or universally accepted definition or identification of what items or goods (tangible or intangible) men are likely to clamour for. Even where these goods are identified, there are differing notions as to the degree of importance or relevance that ought to be attached to each one. A global survey readily shows that while one good is given prominence in one part of the world, it is undermined in some other part or region. It is, therefore, necessary to define at the onset what constitutes these items or goods that man naturally tends to clamour or fight for.

Secondly, we are going to tackle the age-old question of what constitutes a fair distribution of these goods. And thirdly, the relative importance, if any, of each of these items or goods will be examined and related to the entire question of social harmony and stability.

SOCIAL GOODS

What societal goods do men clamour for? Do they end with economic wealth as certain writers tend to advocate or do they go beyond economics? To answer these questions, we need to delve a little into the elements of social stratification.

In every society it is common to find some men who are regarded as 'superior' while the others are regarded as 'inferior'. Very often, there are distinctions between higher and lower, richer and poorer, powerful and powerless individuals, etc. These categorizations together constitute the substance of social stratification. Except, perhaps, where everybody lives at a bare subsistence level, some people are always better-off than others. And from the fact that different individuals possess different abilities, desires and drives, it appears that even if all men were reduced to the same level economically, socially and otherwise, some form of differential development is bound to set in with time.

Social stratification is so complex and multi-faceted that categorization is mainly a tool for analytic studies rather than concrete domains in themselves. Although different people view stratification from different angles, three broad categories are generally discernible and widely accepted. These are known as CLASS, POWER, and STATUS. Although these arose from different sources, phenomena and criteria, they are usually closely related "and one of the central problems in the study of social stratification is the nature and extent of their relationships".[1]

1. El Chinoy, *Society, An Introduction to Sociology*, 2nd Edition, Random House, New York, 1967, p. 168.

CLASS

Class is usually associated with groups of people occupying the same economic position in society and may be defined "as a number of persons sharing a common position in the economic order".[2]

The existence and history of class is an old one, dating back probably to the earliest period of man's civilization. Aristotle, for instance, noted that there are "three elements" in all states: one class is very rich, another very poor and the third is average.[3] Marx defined classes in terms of their relationship to property, distinguishing; among those whose sources of income are from wage-labour, those from capital and those from land.[4] In that analysis, the capitalists were supposed to represent the rich class while land-owners and wage-labourers represented the middle and poor classes respectively.

Although the validity of this analysis in the times of Marx may not be disputed, its application in modern times has been blurred for a number of reasons. First is the emergence of the managerial cadre in modern capitalist economy whose members may own little in terms of property but who are, all the same, powerful in terms of both the power they exercise and their earning capabilities.

Second is the modern form of ownership (of means of production) based on the widely dispersed medium of stock ownership which blurs the dividing line between the capitalist and the labourer by simultaneously making one man a capitalist and a wage-earner. And thirdly, are the modifications in land laws (lease-hold to free-hold, etc.) in different countries over the

2. Ibid. Pg. 171
3. Ibid pg. 169
4. Kari Marx, Capital, III, translated from the 1st German Ed, by Ernest Untermann, Kerr, Chicago, 1909.

years which have *underplayed* the concept of land ownership and land-rent as criteria for defining a social class. Hence, it is now widely accepted that being self-employed (i.e. owning some form of productive property) does not necessarily qualify an individual for the rich class. Skilled labourers, managers, etc., who though may own little or no means of production, might well be found very high in the economic order by virtue of their earning power.

One lesson one learns from a close study of classes, is that men who occupy similar positions in the economic scale are very likely to face identical problems and experiences, and therefore, develop similar interests and attitudes especially in societal or group affairs. As such, in the daily struggle for existence and influence, members of one class, in the course of defending or protecting their class interests, are likely to coalesce. Even when a class remains only a social category, lacking group consciousness or organised structure, the fact that its members may act in roughly the same way, like in voting together and exhibiting similar social attitude, makes class – its nature and study very important in the societal process, and therefore, in figuring the true meaning or nature of equitability.

The relevance of class to the benefits derivable by an individual in a society is immense and variegated. Class position determines not only what one may wear or eat but also what type of house one can live in, what type of transportation facilities are available to him and generally what degree of leisure he can hope to enjoy. It partly determines the type of persons he would associate with and the reciprocation he could reasonably expect from them.

Indeed, even his self-esteem is partly dependent on what class he belongs to. Thus, it is widely believed that the higher the class a man belongs to, the higher his chances of living the 'good life'. Put in another way, class position partly determines the degree of contentment a man can have on earth. And since every normal man seeks maximum contentment, it stands to reason that every person is likely to make every possible effort (legitimate and sometimes, illegitimate) to belong to the higher classes, i.e. to want to possess a lot of money and/ or economic power.

From the foregoing, we can easily deduce that the pursuit and acquisition of wealth is a natural and legitimate aspiration of each normal member of the society, and that the instinct, desire or propensity to struggle for economic advantage is one of the fundamental rights of man. In this sense, therefore, we can say that class-position may be regarded as a social good. For it represents something so dear to man that he has to work, scramble, clamour and if necessary, fight for it. However, for the sake of simplicity we shall continue to refer to this social good as CLASS.

POWER

Power may be defined as the capacity of one person to control the action of others as well as resist such control from others. There is also the frequently correlative phenomenon, authority, which applies to societally recognised right to command in specific areas. Although many roles and statuses carry with them some prescriptive authority or approved freedom to command in certain areas that may affect the actions or behaviours of others, our primary focus here is on political power because of its over-riding effect on almost all other forms of power. Public office holders possess the power and authority for enacting and/or enforcing laws that can affect all facets of societal activities, and also determine what individuals must do or must not do. Furthermore, the fact that the state possesses the legal monopoly of force in all modern societies, makes all other forms of power and authority presumably subject to political control.[5]

So encompassing is the influence of political power on society and the lives of its individual members that almost everyone desires some form of power not only to exert obedience on his fellows but also to forestall others influencing him. A successful politician, for instance, enjoys a unique opportunity to make or influence decisions that affect, directly or indirectly, the lives of others, as well as his own fate. As such, the struggle for power is a very keen aspect of all societies, whether totalitarian or democratic, and the higher the power attached to any particular role or office, the higher the intensity with which people are inclined Èo compete for such a position.

These luring aspects of power then underscore the desire to participate in the political process or to seek political office as a natural and legitimate aspiration of any man. In fact, this is what makes political liberty or the freedom to political participation part of a man's fundamental rights. In this sense, therefore, we may regard political power as yet another social good because, like class, it is something so relevant to the totality of a man's "life chance"[6] that he has to scramble, work, clamour and sometimes, fight for it.

As a result of the foregoing, the mode of power distribution in any society becomes one of the crucial factors influencing the health of that society. Put another way, the type of institutions set up by society to supervise the distribution of political power and the method of determining and changing what role an individual can perform in the political arena, become very important factors vis-a-vis equity and what degree of peace and unity is achievable.

5. El Chinoy, *Society*, Op. cit. p. 175.

6. Life Chance" – an expression used by El Chinoy to describe – in his words "the opportunity to secure the things valued by society – income, goods, power, prestige etc. See — *Society, An Introduction to Sociology*, El Chinoy. Random House, New York, 2nd Ed. 1967. Page 171.

STATUS

We are often reminded by sociologists that wealth and power are not the only criteria with which men assess one another. Such seemingly intangible criteria as family, life style, sex, age, etc., provide alternative or additional bases for social ranking. The system of status – the ranking of roles and their incumbents – constitutes, therefore, another dimension of social stratification. Roles, for instance, vary in the prestige they carry and the reward they provide depending on the authority they carry, their relative importance, the number of persons capable of performing the requisite tasks, and so on.

Although empirical studies of status-ranking often make use of occupation as the chief index of status, it is by no means the only attribute or even the most vital. The importance of any one aspect is a matter of circumstance. The family, for instance, provides the initial or immediate status rank for a child and often forms a very important basis for his future ranking.

However, no matter the empirical characteristics or accepted prerequisites of status, it normally must be ratified by behaviour.

Of the many statuses men may occupy, we may distinguish those based on ASCRIPTION and those based on ACHIEVEMENT. An ascribed status derives from those attributes over which a person has no control, e.g. sex, age, family, tribe, colour, etc. A female remains a female no matter whether she dislikes being one or not and there is nothing she can do to alter it. On the other hand, an achieved status is based "upon qualities or attributes that can be gained only by some direct action – or luck."[7] One must, for instance, pass through or graduate from law school to be a lawyer or must marry to become a husband or wife.

7.   Ibid. p. 172

In primitive societies, ascription is the main or major mode of status-ranking especially with respect to assignment of roles. Leadership is, for instance, by inheritance or succession with a father passing the throne to his own child or children. In the Indian-Caste structure for example, society practically determined what role and, therefore, reward a person must carry out depending on what caste he is born to. His abilities or capabilities are not considered. On the other hand, status-ranking by achievement is mainly an attribute of modem societies.

Again, the status that men carry or are identified with, provides another basis for the determination of the liberties and perquisites each man may enjoy. The higher the status occupied by an individual the higher his chances of enjoying more liberties, leisure and other societal perquisites. In other words, the occupation of higher statuses contributes positively to the realisation of the good life. And since we have already established that the pursuit of the good life is a natural and legitimate concern of the average man, it can also be said that the tendency on the part of each member of society to work towards improving his status (at least the non-*ascriptive* aspect) is also a fundamental right. In fact, it is part of his civic liberty. Thus, status becomes the third and final social good in our analysis.

ESSENTIAL PROPERTIES OF FAIR DISTRIBUTION

From the foregoing, three social goods, namely; Class (or economic power), Power and Status have been identified as the principal attributes of social stratification. We are also led to understand that these three social goods are what men are inclined to clamour or fight for, and that a man's 'life chance" is largely a function of what quantity or quality of each of these items he possesses. We are also led to believe that when men judge the totality of an individual's social worth, they make use of these three criteria. Hence, the man who scores high on all three criteria inevitably appears on the top of the social scale and is accordingly treated. Conversely, those who score low on these counts, of course, find themselves at the bottom of the social scale, and so have to face the unfortunate consequences. Thus, the drive to escape the unpleasant and dire consequences of lagging behind or remaining at the bottom of the social ladder gives men the added impetus to carry on the daily toil and struggle that characterise existence. In the parlance of the modern psychologist, the quest for respectability remains one of the motivating forces behind life.

However, because men differ from one another in their capacities for work, desires and drives, as we pointed out earlier, it follows that not every man will attain and stay at the top of the ladder. In other words, some people must be high on the social scale while some must occupy lowly positions. All these are ways of saying that stratification or gradation (of individuals) is natural to any group or society. If we accept this basic assumption, then we can get on with the real issue: the proper nature of that gradation.

Depending on the rules established by society for the competition implied above, the proportion of people that find themselves either on the high or on the low side of the social scale varies within the society. This, in turn, generates different reactions or responses from members of the society. Where the rules are such as to help place only a few individuals high up on the social scale and the majority at the bottom, we may then witness the incidence of widespread bitterness and contempt for that system by the majority of its members. This, in turn, could cause some members – acting individually or in groups – to side-step the established rules in their desperate bid to achieve success.

Put in another way, these people may resort to criminal or

illegitimate ways in their pursuit of the good life. Where a majority of the inhabitants of that society turns against the established rules or order in an organised fashion, then a social movement, rather than isolated deviant behaviours, would result. Ultimately, social change may result. That is, a change of the existing or earlier rules.

Needless to add, the change can come about peacefully or, where there is sufficient resistance to peaceful change, it can come through violent means or revolution. Thus, we can conclude that peace and social stability are partly dependent on how properly the social goods of a society are divided among its citizens. For it is the response of man to the facts of stratification that partly leads to patterned behaviour which goes on to determine social structure.[8]

We can see from the above that the perceived weakness in the distribution of social goods partly accounts for the incidence of strife and chaos in societies. This leads directly to the questions as to what constitutes a fair distribution of these social goods in a society? That is to say, when does the distribution of social goods best assure the realisation of healthy social ends?

Those who interpreted fair distribution of economic power in terms of equal pay or remunerations for everybody regardless of role or skill are often forced by the consequences of such a policy in real life to re-think their stand. They are confounded by the very fact that differential pay or remuneration constitutes the most lasting and effective method of inducing or creating incentives for acquisition of skills, increasing outputs, accepting authority and responsibility, etc. On the other hand, where differential income or remunerations are pushed up to a position of virtual concentration of economic power or wealth in a few

---

8. Social Structure — Defined by El Chinoy as the organised system of roles and statuses that define relations among groups and individuals'. Ibid. Page 471.

hands, the result has always been negative to social aesthetics and political order.

With respect to political power, it must be emphasised that those who favour absolute freedom of individuals from any form of control by others or a constituted authority are only preaching false equality and, hence, anarchy. On the other hand, the apostles of concentration of power have often found themselves confounded by the inevitable abuse of such powers by their custodians. What is more, the usual unwillingness to obey orders, coupled with violent efforts by the ruled in such circumstances and societies to overthrow the rulers, reminds one of the inherent weaknesses of concentration. Strictly speaking, power that rests on naked force or is concentrated on a few individuals is by nature of things, unstable and transient.

With these points in mind, one is led to conclude that since both extremes (concentration and absolute lack of it) are defective, the ideal must be a compromise position corresponding to the gradation or stratification that is most acceptable to the majority of the members of the society.

In order to appreciate the nature of this compromise, it is considered necessary to apply some statistical concepts known as *normal distribution* and *skewed distribution*.

Normal Distribution

Statisticians use the term "normal" to describe anything or event that exists or occurs in its natural or unbiased form. Thus, a normal distribution is that distribution which, for all practical purposes, appears natural and unbiased. The graph is shown in Figure 1 below. The graph is a bell-shaped curve, also known as the Gaussian curve. But this leads us to the ideal frequency curve as shown below (Fig. 2), the one that is perfectly symmetrical. It is known as the normal distribution curve.

FREQUENCY OF EACH 10-MARK GROUP

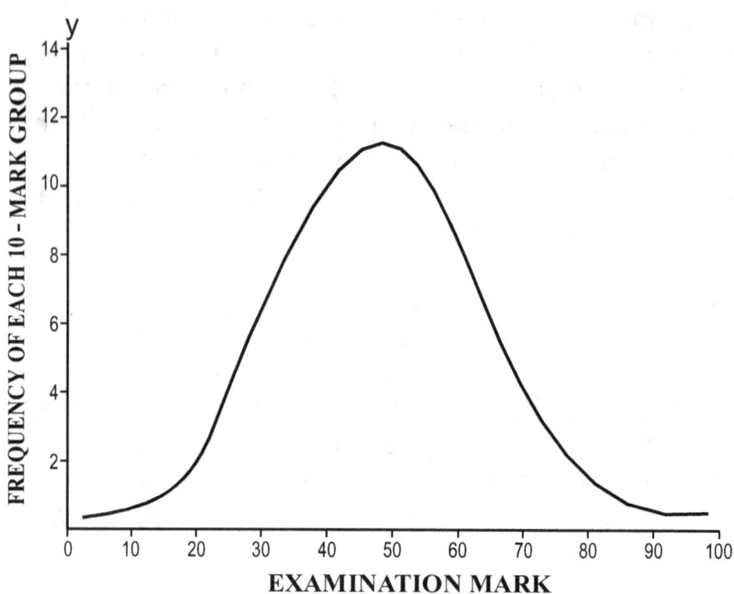

FIGURE 1: FREQUENCY DISTRIBUTION CURVE

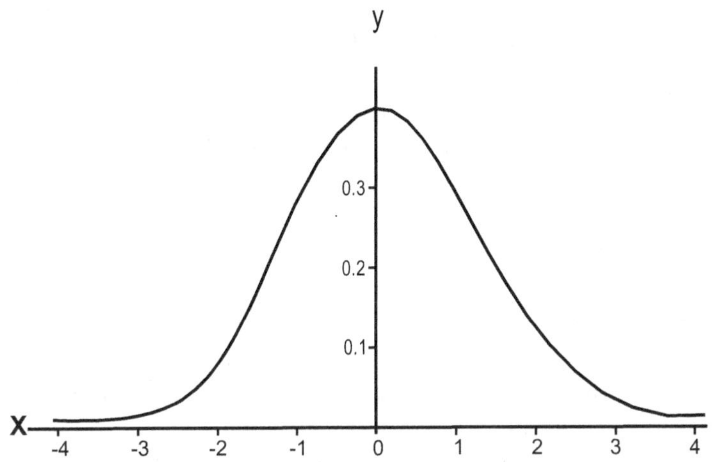

Fig. (2)   THE NORMAL DISTRIBUTION CURVE

$$y = \frac{1}{\sqrt{(2\pi)}}\, e^{-\frac{1}{2}x^2}$$

One major underlying condition for obtaining normal distribution curves is that the population being measured must be homogeneous or unbiased. For instance, when you construct the frequency distribution curve of chest measurements of young men in a certain age range in a given community (for purposes of sewing jackets for them), you are likely to find that the frequency distribution curve will attune to normal distribution especially if the population is large enough. In contrast, a skewed distribution results from non-homogenous population.

Skewed Distribution

Now, let us imagine what would have happened in the most unlikely situation in which Forms III and V students are merged together to take an examination meant for Form V students only. Quite clearly, the Form III students would be placed in a position of disadvantage having not been prepared, like their Form V counterparts, for that level of examination. This will reflect in the results sheet recording of a large number of students with extremely low marks and a very small number of students with extremely high marks. This is said to be skewed on the positive side and may be represented by the curve shown in figure 3(a) below. It should be noticed that the curve is far from being symmetrical and hence from being normal.

The complement of this curve will occur if the examination had been set for Form III students with the Form V students as invitees to take part. Many with a large number of high marks and few with very low marks, a condition referred to as negatively skewed distribution, and depicted in figure 3(b), is likely to occur.

A skewed distribution curve should, therefore, be seen as a graphical representation of a distribution in which the set of conditions is biased or loaded against or in favour of some numbers of the population that is being observed. It is patently an abnormal type of distribution which relies on a method that fails to guarantee equality of opportunity.

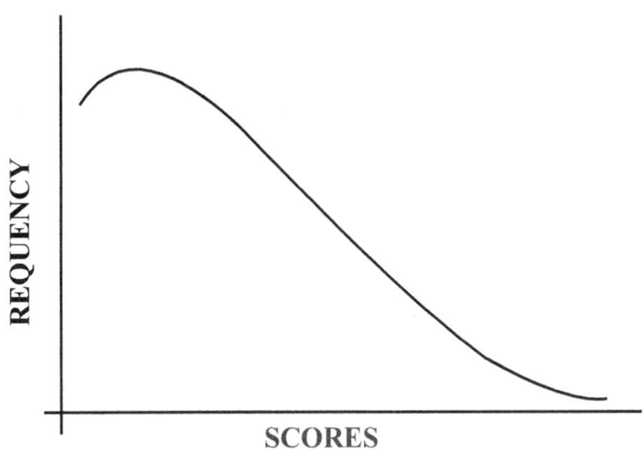

Fig. 3a. **POSITIVELY SKEWED DISTRIBUTION**

Fig. 3b. **NEGATIVELY SKEWED DISTRIBUTION**

Significance of the Normal and Skewed Distribution Patterns

Because schools and colleges normally permit only the students of the same class to sit the same examination, the students usually produce results that follow the normal distribution pattern. And unless there are artificial attempts to manipulate results, every student would accept his or her result as a fair indication of his performance.

From the foregoing, it can be deduced that a normal distribution of any item (tangible or intangible) among the individual members of a society is least likely to bring about any serious opposition and disapproval. In other words, it is the fairest mode of distribution possible in this imperfect world.

Furthermore, normal distribution shows a fluidity in ranking which abhors compact categorization. There is absence of rigid lines of separation from the various levels of stratification. This means that where a society is so stratified, there would be the least likelihood for people to develop undue class-consciousness – which is why we consider it the optimal point or the midway between concentration and absolute lack of it, and, therefore, a vital property (as far as distribution is concerned) of a true egalitarian society.

In summary, we would like to re-emphasise that for the distribution of economic power among individuals in a society to be deemed fair or equitable, such distribution must exhibit the following properties:

i) The frequency curve of the distribution must tend to normal. That is to say, that the averagely rich individuals or group must constitute the modal group with the number of richer and poorer individuals diminishing in relatively equal proportions from that point on either side of the modal group. That is, the eventual number of excessively rich or excessively poor individuals within the society is relatively small.

ii) That the income distribution among the various economic strata must reflect the properties of the normal distribution curve.

With respect to the distribution of political power and status position, normalcy in distribution can hardly be expressed quantitatively as one does when handling more tangible items like economic power. However, a prudent qualitative analysis can readily give us a fair idea of what form of government is best suited in guaranteeing a semblance of normalcy in the distribution of power among individuals in a society or nation as well as between nations, as we shall see in chapters 6 and 7. As for Status position and its distribution, this is virtually always reflected from Class and Power positions or distribution.

So in a nutshell, the above depict about what the centrist ideology is anchor on.

Although further attributes of an egalitarian society may be anchored on such varied factors as Education, Religion, Judicial and Legal Institutions, Science and Technology, absence of Cultural Imperialism and Ethnocentrism, availability of employment and their distribution, productivity, etc., they can only be used as supportive facts to the above.

PART II
SOCIO-ECONOMIC FORMA

CHAPTER 3

EXAMINING NIGERIA'S SOCIO-ECONOMIC CHALLENGES

Most often analysis of Nigeria's social and economic conditions or lack of well-being focuses almost entirely on the role or contribution of government and political leaderships to that state of affairs. We generally tend to lose sight of the crippling input made by other forms of leadership to the nation's socioeconomic failure. I am talking about the contribution of the nation's captains of industry, pioneer and leading entrepreneurs, etc. to the malady. A close examination readily reveals that the extent to which the national economy is compromised at these lower levels is indeed enormous and ought to be taken into consideration by any genuine attempt at resolving and reversing the trends that have brought the society and economy to their present sorry pass.

Indeed, in so far as macroeconomic aggregates subsume the aggregation of decisions and activities at the micro-level, any pretensions at solving or proffering solutions to Nigeria's problems without paying adequate attention to the occurrences at the lower strata, at the level of companies and individual economic behaviour, will completely miss the target. Our study shows that Nigeria's commercial, professional and industrial leaderships have not been as visionary and as creative as they ought to be. To a large extent, it is the economic collapses which occur within their scope of operation and influence, at the micro-levels, that manifest at the national scale and have largely led to the persistent cycles of massive corruption and economic stagnation that have become the lot of the Nigerian system for quite some time.

The contribution of the private sector of the Nigerian establishment to the dismal performance of the economy is best analysed using the professionals or professional groupings as index. We are referring to the style and modus operandi of our doctors, architects, engineers, accountants, pharmacists, lawyers, etc. It is noteworthy that one of the chief characteristics of Nigerian professionals is the trend towards fragmentation and the establishment of one-man practices. In Nigeria today, virtually every qualified professional architect, engineer, pharmacist, lawyers, etc., is a firm by himself.

This should be contrasted with the trend in most other parts of the world where it is common to find professional firms with very large pools of professional men and women making up each firm or corporate practice. In virtually all the developed economies, emerging markets and the seriously upwardly mobile developing countries most professional groups or firms usually consist of upwards of scores and hundreds of professionals. You would find, for instance, big law firms with up to one thousand or more lawyers, all working together and under one single corporate leadership; ditto for architects, engineers, etc.

The advantage of the latter kind of set-up, collocation or clustering together is that there is synergy, specialisation even within the profession, cross fertilisation of ideas, research and economy of scale. This is a recipe for efficiency, optimum performance and progress. Indeed, this is what organisation is about! It is well known that usually each professional man tends to be very good in particular branches of the profession and not so good in some others. There are really very few all-rounders.

Thus, some architects, for instance, are either good in design, detailing, presentation, site works or supervision, contract management or job letting, etc., or a combination of a number of these or other aspects of the professional duties of the architect. Large professional architectural firms thus have the potential of being made up of 'experts' in virtually all the branches and aspects of the professional calling. On the face of it therefore, the large firm is in a better position to handle any professional job and assignment more efficiently and successfully than a small group or one-man firm.

It is these successes that are recorded at the micro-levels, at the level of companies and firms by such large and organised groups that translate into the economic success and development that manifest at the macro-level, at the level of society and nation. In contrast, the failures, inefficiency and poorly conceived and shoddily executed projects that characterise small professional groups or one- man firms, translate to dismal economic performances that seem to have become part and parcel of 'unorganised' societies and countries like Nigeria.

Have you stopped to imagine or contemplate how the many one-doctor clinics and hospitals that dot the Nigerian landscape and healthcare delivery industry manage - say, during surgery? Well, the picture is that you would in a generality of cases, have the single in-house doctor act the part of the surgeon, aesthetician, technician or controller of the oxygen cans and other equipment, bio-chemist, pharmacist, administrator of all the myriad operations that go with surgery all by himself and, perhaps with the aid of a few ill-qualified, ill-motivated and inexperienced nurses. With that kind of scenario, does it surprise anybody that these one-doctor hospitals have very few successful operations or surgery; that they indeed constitute slaughter houses in which innumerable patients get butchered every now and then. So to recap, the failures recorded by these outfits constitute one of the drawbacks that have kept Nigeria's healthcare delivery system in the doldrums.

It can be shown that the picture painted above of the one-man architectural firm or the one-doctor hospital in Nigeria could be replicated and likened to the operations of the other numerous one-man professional outfits in Nigeria, be it in engineering practice and the ill-network of roads, public drains or other line-systems they design and supervise; in accountancy and their shoddy and fraudulent audit reports; in law practice and the innumerable un-researched ill-conceived advocacies; and the rest of them. It is all a catalogue of dismal failures at the micro-levels that have ultimately translated to collapses at the macro-level or the level of nation and society.

It is not only that these small practices do not have the right depth of staff to generate the right professional advice and work, they also cannot muster the right resources to acquire the needed tools and equipment, books, professional journals, etc. that should keep them in line with the latest developments and new concepts in any of the professional callings. Little wonder then that they can hardly perform, help themselves and make the requisite contribution expected from them to our social, economic, technological, and even political progress.

What are the unique factors that have tended to detract the Nigerian professionals from the corporate track commonly trodden by their counterparts in other parts of the world? What are those peculiarities of the Nigerian professionals that seemingly make them so different from professionals from other lands? Again, we prefer to seek the answers from the micro-levels. The truth is that historically the Nigerian pioneer and leading professionals who more or less took over from the expatriate professional firms did not take care of the younger generation of (Nigerian) professionals that came later or that served under them.

In their general drive to 'maximise' profit, the pioneers and leading professionals threw the standards established by white men or the colonialist expatriates they replaced overboard and began to appropriate virtually all incomes made by the new firms to themselves, leaving peanuts for the retinue of employed fellow professionals and other sundry staff that work under them even when these employees work on multi-million dollar projects which attract huge fees for the firm.

In fact, these corporate leaders are known to determine the salaries of their employees based on the notion that they should and would be collecting huge sums of money from whatever contractor or companies they supervise or superintend over as 'gifts'. This generally forces the younger professional to depend on the contractors' hand-outs for virtually all his livelihood. And being thus compromised, the project suffers, for as the saying goes, there is no free lunch. It is this kind of in-built corruption that account for shoddy jobs and the lowering of standards that is so commonplace in Nigeria. The scenario is also typified in the civil service where too many people are employed but paid such mean salaries that they become permanently and perpetually corruption-prone.

It is in fact woe betide thee for any of these young professionals or employees that refuses to toe the line; to feed from the filthy lucre offered by those individuals or companies he superintends over, for it is his bosses, colleagues, even relatives and 'friends' that will bury him alive and dance on top of his grave for his mere non-compliance with the subsisting system in operation – to say nothing about the excruciating impact of the poor salary and wages on which he is signed on. Given that scenario, it can be said that in Nigeria, corruption is compelling, and will remain so for as long as the status quo persists.

The above scenario should be contrasted with what obtains among some internationally-linked business outfits where some level of prudence and fairness in distributive standards – the so-called 'international standards of ethics' – prevail. We are talking about what is witnessed among some of the foreign oil companies and suchlike that do business in Nigeria. Here, different rules appear to operate. We find that in generality of cases, many Nigerians who work for such companies refuse to accept hand-outs from contractors and professional groups that work for them or handle their consultancy briefs. But this, as many of such individuals would say, is because they are well paid by the companies they work for and therefore do not need to 'palm' such 'gifts' or 'hand-outs'. But these are Nigerians nonetheless.

Therefore, it is safe to conclude that what makes the difference is the system. And that the persistence of corruption as witnessed in the earlier scenario is patently systemic. The average Nigerian young professional is therefore more of a victim of the system than the happy exploiter of it. Indeed, many feel quite humiliated by the status quo, and some do try to extricate themselves from that system; to shorn a beggarly existence and perpetual manipulation by (or collusion with) contractors, or clients in the case of accountants, auditors, etc.

Movement of Individualism & Enthronement of Anarchy

Historically, the above subsisting Nigerian system has led to fragmentation of professional firms across the board. Being thus humiliated and short-changed by the system, most of the younger Nigerian professionals predictably move out from the established firms to seek solace in the establishment of smaller groups and/or one-man outfits. Before you knew it, a pattern emerged in which younger Nigerian professionals moved on or were expected to establish their own professional firms as soon as they pass their professional practice exams or immediately after pupillage, hence the emergence of the unique degenerate Nigerian system and professional ethics or culture discussed above, in which each qualified professional virtually becomes a firm of his own. That culture is one of incipient disorganisation and anarchy.

As the number of firms in any one professional group mushroomed, the practitioners inevitably began to undercut one another in order to remain afloat. The rules of professional conduct and all the extant regulation that should guide professional practice were virtually jettisoned and compromised by the day. In Nigeria today, we have degenerated to a level where one professional would, in collusion with government officials steal a proposal submitted to government by another professional group, erase the name of that firm from the document, affix his own imprint, resubmit same, collect the contract and smile to the banks without any repercussion for these dastardly unprofessional conduct. In Nigeria today, integrity hardly counts, nor is professional competence of much consequence. All these have in turn ravaged the professions leading to paralysis and the collapses of most professional groups, large or small.

Meanwhile, the predictably derisory services offered by the inadequately staffed, ill-funded and withering local firms and companies became manifest and unbearable. The trend has partially created the loophole for foreign professional groups and companies to recapture the commanding heights of professional practice in the country. It has reasserted the "white hand-can-do-it" syndrome in virtually all areas of professional practice in the country, be it in engineering design and construction, accountancy and architecture. Many projects or contracts are now being let out as turn-key projects in which foreign groups and companies handle everything from design to construction and even furnishing and interior decor. Examples include the construction of the nation's National Assembly Complex, the multi-billion naira Abuja

National Stadium Complex and of course innumerable important projects in the private sector, especially in the nation's fledgling oil industry.

The Nigerian medical system with its ill-equipped, ill-staffed hospitals, public or private, is side-tracked by those who can afford to go abroad for even the slightest of afflictions. But for the expected insurmountable difficulties the nation's judicial and legal systems pose for the foreigner or the uninitiated, foreign lawyers and legal practitioners would have invaded and taken over legal advocacies offered by the lucrative litigation-prone Nigerian environment. Did the Federal Government of Nigeria not hire a team of foreign lawyers to research into and represent her at the World Court in our dispute with Cameroun over the ownership of the oil-rich Bakassi Peninsula?

Obviously, one of the reasons for that action was that no local legal firm was thought to possess the manpower and research capability and resources to corner such a lucrative contract or brief. In the same vein, it appears, no local accounting firm is thought large enough to possess the capacity to audit big government parastatals like the NNPC. The pre-shipment inspection agents that inspect imports coming into the fatherland at about one per cent of the value of these imports as fee must not be Nigerians, if for no other reason, because Nigerian professionals have not been able to build any agency or firms that can boast of the staffing and other resources to undertake such assignments. So, we have to pay huge scarce foreign exchange resources to get foreigners to perform these otherwise simple tasks for us.

One obvious and damaging consequence of the above trend is that government's presumed attempts to reflate the economy by the award of huge road construction and other contracts have ended up being dismal failures because the multi-national companies that get these contracts repatriate virtually all the disproportionately large proceeds while their local counterparts similarly siphon whatever they get abroad for savings and investment in the more stable economies of the Western world. For under the prevailing system, they get away with paying the local labourers and employees that work under their supervision just enough to keep body and soul together.

This then obviates and obstructs the trickle-down effect that should have put more money into the hands of Nigerians through the quantum of solid and substantial earnings expected to accrue to the skilled and unskilled workers in the nation's service sector. The effect is to prolong the economic depression that has been with us for so long by stagnating consumer purchasing power and disposable incomes of the masses of Nigerian citizens.

Indeed, in recent times, many leading Nigerian professional architects and engineers have turned into portfolio consultants. They no longer maintain offices and staff nor do they bother to make use of (younger) Nigerian professionals and draughtsmen as employees in the execution of lucrative design schemes and briefs that come their way. Rather, the practice today is to hop over to Ghana where they engage Ghanaian consultants and professional groups in the execution, design, detailing and drafting of the assigned projects, and of course pay cheaply in grossly devalued cedi, the Ghanaian currency.

In the meantime, many young Nigerian graduate-professionals are left without work and avenues to imbibe needed professional ethos and practical training. It is clear that if this trend continues, then in the near future, the professional instincts of jobless Nigerian graduate-professionals will be atrophied; many will turn to trading and crime, and national professional and technological know-how will be the worse for it.

It is regrettable that some senior Nigerian professionals who have been exposed and are knowledgeable about developments and professional practice in the more advanced countries of the world could allow themselves to embrace the odd notion that there are too many professionally trained people in Nigeria. Trained architects in Nigeria for instance number less than ten thousand. In some of the developed economies, that number would make up just about three or four architectural firms. Sadly, in Nigeria, they would represent thousands of firms.

The picture in other professions conforms to the above model. But rather than see the problem in the available number of firms, Nigeria's professional leaders prefer or pretend to see the problem in terms of available number of individual professionals! Thus instead of devising measures to mollify the alienated younger professionals, they cast off in the opposite direction and adopt measures that further alienate and frustrate the younger members of the professions, creating chaos and untold upheavals and declines in social, economic and political aesthetics of the nation.

But the above synthesis is not limited to the professions. The model is applicable to all private sector players and operators in the Nigerian economy, be they in the commercial, industrial or agricultural sectors. The winner-takes-all syndrome painted for professionals above is noticeable in the myriad trading, manufacturing, agricultural and other establishments or sectors of the economy. There is a systemic process and propensity for those at the helm to corner a disproportionate size of company incomes or added-value to themselves and leave a pittance to the mass of hired hands and labourers that are used in running these organisations.

A survey of factor-shares in Nigeria's quoted or public liability companies clearly underscores this point. Most of these companies devoted less than 30% of their added-value to the payment of salaries and wages and general staff welfare. This is to say nothing of undeclared incomes that do not come under the purview of distribution between the factors – labour and capital.

The situation is even worse in the private or limited liability companies and in the so-called informal sector where generally speaking one man represents or functions both as chairman and managing director of a company as well as its board of directors. Here anything goes, and really nobody is there to call the chief executive officer, CEO, to account for anything, either in terms of taking good care of employees, paying adequate salaries and wages or even in terms of paying commensurate tax to state coffers.

When these occurrences are put down in a generalised fashion, people might and do get the impression that the situation is exaggerated. But we have come across several instances of this discouraging practice on the part of established Nigerian business organisations that could startle anybody.

About ten years ago, we came across a letter of employment emanating from a renowned law firm in which a qualified lawyer and university graduate of nearly ten years' post-graduate experience was being offered a basic salary of N3,000.00 a month with various allowances making up a total of N10,000.00 gross monthly pay package, to work six-days a week in the company.

Many graduate school teachers earn less than N6,000.00 per month, all-found, to teach in many of the growing number of private schools that actually make a killing in their line of business; that derive fantastic revenues from the army of Nigerian parents and guardians that are so eager to pull their wards out of the deteriorating Nigerian public schools. This is at a time when the stipulated minimum wage in the country was put at N18,000.00 per month for unskilled workers.

Indeed, Governments' attempts to bolster the take-home pay of workers have been less than effective for a number of reasons. One, such stipulations are hardly adhered to in the private sector. Two, in the areas where such is respected and upheld, like the civil service, these pegged rates are usually quickly overtaken over time by developments in the economy, especially in comparison to increases in national income or productivity.

Now if the above salary offer was coming from some low-level company battling to stay afloat, the offer would not cause any consternation or surprise anybody. But the Law firm alluded to above and its subsidiaries were leaders in the industry and were known to be making a killing in the field. Its proprietor was one of the nation's leading light, a social and human rights crusader who ought to know the overall impact and implication of this kind of salary structure on the economic and other rights of the recipient and the Nigerian economy as a whole.

As a highly successful firm, the company could afford to pay a lot more than it was offering. But the instinct to maximise profit in an environment with a glut of qualified applicants and job-seekers appears to be the restraining factor. With this scenario, it appears that the hope of reflating the Nigerian economy via the so-called trickle-down effect, in which large firms and/or generous recipients of high incomes and government contracts are expected to better the earnings of their employees, will never come about.

In the Nigerian informal sector, the notorious one-man business syndrome is most pronounced. Take the traders and the array of semi-skilled artisans, welders, plumbers, motor mechanics, for instance. There is little effort on the part of this social category to forge medium or large-scale organisations, to build economies of scale, trading conglomerates and such like; structures that can muster the resources that would ensure sustainable and promising future and leverage for the company, and that would cushion its members against risks and unforeseen bad times and hence enhance the quality of life of its members.

Rather, what we see is the same propensity on the part of leading members of this group to build one-man empires, short-change their employees, associates and appropriate virtually every income to themselves. Again, the result has been the kind of fragmentation prevalent among the professionals. It is a situation that, for the traders, produces honeycomb market structures and myriad tiny squalid windowless market stalls where these traders display their odd wares and engage in cut-throat competition and petty frauds. This should be contrasted with the modern emergent mega-shopping facilities and department stores that have become a permanent and endearing feature of progressive nations of the world.

In all the more progressive states of the world, what we see or what transpires virtually by the day are mergers of giant corporations to produce even larger groups and combines. The new emergent mega-companies are then able to pool together more resources to carry out new and intricate research, patent new inventions and create new wealth and fantastic fortunes. In Nigeria on the other hand, the general trend is towards ruptures and disintegration into smaller ineffective and unproductive groups.

Conversely, Nigeria's pinnacle of wealth is not peopled by men that have patented any inventions nor even earned their riches through copyright in artistic or any other form of intellectual work. Rather the majority of the country's men of riches are people who made their money through government either as contractors, suppliers or through dubious deals and swindling, grand larceny and outright embezzlements. It is a process that impoverishes the masses and breeds more and more corruption, indolence, and dependence on crude petroleum resources that Nigerians do not even tap or mine by themselves. This truncates societal values and work-ethic, erodes and whittles the authority of those in government to the extent that there is acute erosion of authority and they virtually have to fall back to naked force to get things done.

Parlous Economy & Social Disintegration

The cumulative effect of the above build-ups can be easily enumerated. First, there is a mammoth concentration of national resources in fewer and fewer hands that have practically wiped off the middle class in the country. (Nigeria is now said to have one of the world's highest levels of inequality; its Gini co-efficient is put close to 0.6. Of course with that level of inequality most people are untouched by economic development as most increases in income accrue to those who are already rich).

Secondly, there is a dangerously depreciating disposable income and purchasing power for a large proportion of the populace. Thirdly, mass unemployment and a process of internal marginalisation that has been grinding away the foundations of society are evident everywhere. Fourthly, public life is marked by financial indiscipline at the workplace and a concomitant endemic corruption in high and low places. Fifthly, the crime waves keep rising.

These then are some of the main factors or manifestations that shape the decidedly parlous Nigerian economy. The low and depreciating purchasing power of consumers has been responsible for poor sales on the part of manufacturers and producers in general, leading as it were, to overflowing inventory in company warehouses, cut-backs in production, retrenchments and general business collapses.

Another remarkable dysfunctional feature of the Nigerian economy is the tendency on the part of owners and captains of industry to import wholesale foreign-built industrial plants and machinery. There is little attempt to have Nigerians design and fabricate machinery and manufacturing plants locally. The persistent attempt by our industry captains to rely solely on foreign technology for Nigeria's industrial production purposes has indeed had a very profound and negative impact on the economy.

In the first place, because these imported technological artefacts are too sophisticated for our stage of development and call for continuous and steady supply of spare parts from the original producers, they constitute a permanent drain of the nation's scarce resources. Even so, Nigerian technicians often have great difficulty in providing the kind of maintenance demanded by these machines and production plants. Invariably, the plants break down and have to be discarded and replaced with new and even more sophisticated models.

Alternatively, foreign engineers and technicians are imported at great cost to fix or repair them. It has in fact been calculated that the cost incurred by Nigerians in importing, repairing and replacing these plants generally outstrip the net value added to the economy by these artefacts. Conversely, the indiscriminate wholesale importation and employment of foreign technology or alien machines and production plants contribute more in the impoverishment of Nigerians than in the economic development of the country.

A case in point is the unending turn-around- maintenance of Nigeria's foreign-built state-owned oil refineries. The project which again is being handled by foreign technical experts is said to have gulped over N 3.5 billion, an amount that could quite easily build new refineries for the country, especially, if handled by local engineers and technicians, for some of these foreign-built refineries are not better than the Biafran-built Amandugba petroleum refinery now of yore. It is arguable whether the actual values added to the nation's economy by these foreign-built refineries are anywhere near the total cost paid by Nigeria for their construction and maintenance over the years.

Secondly, the wholesale employment of foreign technological artefacts by Nigerian manufacturers, construction firms, etc., tends to de-emphasise labour-intensive modes of production and whittle labour incomes. It alienates the masses of abundant and capable human labour resources in the country from the workplace and creates what is generally termed technological unemployment. This adds to the massive unemployment situation in the country and helps swell the rank of retail traders milling around in every nook and cranny of the country virtually stampeding or choking the economy by its sheer size. For what we have is a situation where a disproportionate size of young men and women who should be working in factories, farms, etc., roam the streets in the name of trading or business.

Indeed, in the last few decades, Nigeria has witnessed a geometric rise in the proportion of its populace engaged in the retail trading sub-sector while the proportion of those that could be regarded as producers of any kind of goods have shrunk to a point where Nigeria could be derisively referred to as largely a nation of traders - traders of mainly imported goods. This is a minus for the country, for no great economy can be built through low production at home and a propensity for a great majority of its citizens to turn into importers and sellers of foreign goods.

The third consequence of Nigeria's over-dependence on foreign technological artefacts is that local initiative at the creation of an indigenous technological culture is dampened and permanently stifled. The Biafran revolution had aptly demonstrated that an indigenous black technological civilisation is possible and achievable around here. The absence of such a civilisation in Nigeria today is therefore clearly not inherent in the quality of mankind that inhabit the geographical space called Nigeria, but definitely on the way the country has been managed or mismanaged since the end of the civil war.

Weak and Visionless Political Leadership

Our analysis in the foregoing has tended, on the face of it, to blame the dismal performance of the economy on the actions of company managers, captains of industry and leading members of the business community. The analysis may have given the impression that the problem of efficient and sound national economic management is further complicated by the fact that actors and managers in the economy are many and diverse, pursuing multiple and often mutually opposing objectives. It is not by any means so.

The operators and managers mentioned above only deal at the micro-levels of the economy. National economic management deals with the issues at the macro-level, at the level of national political leadership. It is thus the general duty of government, at the national level, to give overall direction in all matters of economic development. It is the duty of the Federal Government of Nigeria to manipulate the macro-economic variables in such a way as to check any dysfunctional and economically oppressive attitudes and enactments at the micro-levels, to provide overall health to the national economy. But how well has this vital role of government been handled over the years?

The answer to that question is of course located in the perceived and actual state of well-being of the economy itself. Accordingly, it is obvious that governments' efforts in this direction have been less than assiduous and efficacious. Prof Adebayo Adedeji was right when he wrote (June, 2000) "that the first civilian government for 17 years is in danger of losing the battle to cope with its daunting inheritance of mismanagement, corruption and other ravages of military rule; that the mood in the business community [other than the petroleum sector, which was then experiencing a boom] is as gloomy as it has ever been and that while short-run macro-economy has improved as a result of the boom in the oil-sector which has bolstered both the balance-of-payments and budget revenue, the spread effects on the economy as a whole have been negligible".

In other words, he continues, "the non-oil sector of the economy, especially the agricultural and manufacturing sub-sectors, has remained stagnant. The average industrial capacity utilisation in the 1990s was about 30 per cent but last year (1999) even this low capacity utilisation plummeted by almost one-quarter; [varying levels of decline have been witnessed over the following decades]. Growth rate of agricultural output remains one-half of the population's growth rate".

Nigeria's GDP in in June 2017 was 114.0 USD Billion with GDP per capita of about US$570 while the inflation rate hovers around 11 per cent, with population growth rate of about 3 per cent. All this in spite of the boom in the oil sector, which only weakened in 2015! Nigeria has indeed become a by-word for poverty, fraud and misery!!

Meanwhile, with interest or lending rate hovering around 25-30 per cent, it is certain that no sane investor would borrow bank funds to start new manufacturing plants. For the interest rate burden would certainly choke or stifle the investment even before it begins to bear fruit of any kind. Conversely, bank funds in Nigeria today can only be accessed and utilized for the booming import trade and big business.

What is more, the relatively open-door import liberalisation policy of the Nigerian governments (perhaps with the possible exception of the current Buhari government), indeed, the disguised encouragement offered by government to importers, has had a most profound and disruptive impact on the nation's industry and agriculture. With the then spate of massive importation of cheap finished and agricultural goods, local production of equivalent items is made so unattractive and fruitless.

Conversely, local producers were being forced to close shop and join the ranks of traders and distributors of the imported items. These governments could not by any stretch of the imagination pretend that they were not aware that rice producers in Bida, Wukari, Abakaliki and other rice producing centres in the country virtually downed tools or have been muscled out of business because of the unfair competition from the armada of cheap imported rice that have taken over the local Nigerian markets. And that some of those displaced farmhands are now swelling the rank of hoodlums and 'area-boys' that terrorise Nigerian cities and citizenry;

ditto for many factory hands or workers that are equally displaced from the workplace as factories downsize and retrench workers as they increasingly lose more and more of their market-share to cheap foreign goods.

It is most disheartening that the reaction of some of our leaders to the burgeoning crime wave in the country which largely stems from these observable lapses in national economic management has, in the main, been to build many more prisons. In other words, instead of devising strategies to get the rampaging youths back to the factories and the farms, they saw the solution in terms of locking them away in detention camps that would be constructed with funds that ought to have been deployed to create jobs for the obviously marginalised youths.

Indeed, with unemployment running at an estimated 30%, it is quite a wonder that the economy still manages to limp along. The American economy collapsed in 1929 when its unemployment rate hit 25%. It is discernible that but for the extended family system by which the buoyant individual takes care of both his immediate family and also provides reasonable assistance to distant relatives, the Nigerian economy would long have completely crumbled. The Argentine-type December 2001 collapse and chaos would in comparison really have been a child's play as to the level of social banditry, strife and devastation that would have occurred in this country.

No nation can bear for a long time the collapse of its economic foundations without losing the love and loyalty of its citizens. In Nigeria today, it is doubtful whether the sense of a sustaining national purpose still survives. It is equally uncertain whether the zeal and high hopes that accompanied the return of democracy to Nigeria are still in place.

In the light of the above, it is not surprising, and Prof Adedeji agrees with the view, that there is considerable disappointment about the non-actualisation of the so-called democracy dividends. The huge expectation of 1999 about the prospects for the Nigerian economy under civilian leadership and management has begun to yield place to a rising feeling of frustration and even nostalgia for military rule or government.

It is now usual or habitual for analysts and commentators to applaud every government budget projections and policy pronouncements as visionary and efficacious, only to blame the failures that invariable accompany these on what is now dubbed 'poor implementation' of the various budgets and policies. But such facile assumptions really do not tally with realities or facts on the ground. The bane of government's exertions on the economy is located not only on poor implementation as the saying goes, but also on faulty analysis, poor projections and a general lack of vision as to how the economy should be managed for effective and beneficial results.

Economist, Charles Njoku, put his finger on this point when he wrote that:

Starting from the first Economic Summit summoned by Chief Ernest Shonekan, [one] has been pointing at a grievous flaw which has persisted perennially. Our economic woes are legion and the Economic

Summits aggravated this by offering a myriad of remedies to the bewildered immobility of policy makers and implementers. Our true economic salvation lies not in a cornucopia of prescriptions but in a few key ideas that would enable the economy to finally take off. A high jumper jumps highest taking off from one leg and not two feet. A comprehensive scatter of analysis and prescriptions is merely meretricious and not efficacious to development. The recurrent question to the Economic Summit is: What are the two or three central ideas of utmost priority by which the Nigerian economy would make the quantum leap to non-oil dependent, sustained growth and development. The Vision 2010 committee had no answer, neither have the yearly Economic Summits.

Moreover, an economic policy that is predicated on the vain hope of bringing in foreign investors to develop the Nigerian economy is unrealistic. It bears an attitudinal stance that sees economic development as something that can be imported, that can survive or be sustained in spite of the people. It is a policy that if pursued to its logical end, would alienate the people from the mainstream of the economy and put true national development very much in the future.

The right model for our development does not lie in the direction which such analysts point. It lies instead in the use of the energies and the ingenuity of the people in the harnessing and development of the resources which God has so abundantly lavished on us. Contrary to the urgings and permutation, Nigeria cannot be developed without Nigerians.

Nigeria's self-development, the work and welfare of the people must have precedence over the concern for foreign investors and investment. We must look inwards. Our impression is that despite the obvious patriotic inclination of some of these analysts and their exertions, the country's economic and political climate and future remain bleak. But as a Shakespeare character says,

> ... great are the uses of adversity; which though like
> toad, ugly and venomous, wears yet a precious jewel
> on its head.

History is replete with examples of the tragedy that sweeps nations when ancient rivalries and the inertia of habit freeze the scope of decision. Equally, history is marked by some moments when an old order gives way to new patterns. These are times of potential disorder and confusion but also of opportunity for new creation, modernisation and progress. We face such a moment today. If we may quote from Shakespeare's *Julius Caesar* again;

> On such a full sea are we now afloat; And we must
> take the current where it serves. Or lose our ventures.

The speaker goes on to make the well-known generalization:
There is a tide in the affairs of men which, taken at the flood, leads on to fortune; Omitted, all the voyage of their life is bound in shallows and in miseries.

Indeed, the time has come for a visitation; for the enunciation of a philosophy of action that should dislodge this lethargy in us and that would help bring about the much-desired and hoped-for turn-around in our social, economic and political circumstances.

We have been speaking about change, about a transition from one situation to another. The need for change is accepted in every mode of thought, even in the ancient Heraclitian theory of constant flux. It is also clear in the philosophies of Aristotle, Hegel and William James. While the economic predisposition of the past administrations may have served some useful purpose and indeed provided some indisputable respite for this country in the past, the need for the creation of a new and better system of socio-economic management and administration persists. Even the envisaged new order may in the long-run also become outworn and due for change, following the Hegelian law of dialectics. In other words, once any system or philosophy attains its zenith, it will wither and decline. Any attempt to artificially sustain it and forestall its predictable demise would ultimately prove an exercise in futility.

Philosophy or adherence to an authentic one is a valuable asset that is necessary for the survival of a people. A developing nation of today is confronted with the problem of choice between her own indigenous values and the foreign values and attitudes that have been super-imposed on her. Nigeria is one of the nations that face undue pressures of world influences which are sometimes too strong to resist. These pressures which range from the problems of colonisation to those of ethnic and religious heterogeneity and of dependency on foreign nations have left Nigeria either without a national philosophy or with a varied and diversified or confused philosophy which does not address itself to the problems and needs of the citizenry.

Without doubt, the task of salvaging the Nigerian nation from the harried and harrowing experiences of colonial rule, subjugation and foreign domination has been a trying and protracted affair. But despite the obvious delays and circumambiency that have characterised the march, it appears to us that the goal is now in sight.

Our modest assessment is that the journey has undergone two vital stages and is now entering the third and final phase. The first phase came about when the country gained political independence from Britain. The second stage consisted of a period of struggle for competence within the post-colonial environment and essentially under the formats prescribed by our former colonisers and some other dominant external forces. The third stage has to do with the exploitation of indigenous intellectual input in tackling our core developmental and organisational problems.

This aims at evolving new initiatives in institutional super-structure, in the realm of thought and practice, and in sociological, political and economic arrangements. Its highpoint is the actual generation of ideas, systems and processes, and the synthesis of these into an authentic philosophy or programme of action, relevant to our unique circumstance and experience, and whose execution would translate to the rebuilding of our battered social, economic, and political structures.

This boils down to the fact that we have reached a point in history when the evolution and adoption of a genuine, home-grown, critical and pragmatic philosophy of socio-economic and socio-political management have become a sine qua non to the task of sustaining our collective existence and of consolidating the gains and victories won through the years by our forebears. The erroneous myth that modern Africa's intellectual dwelling place is in the West's second- hand shop has to be finally repudiated and laid to rest.

Only an honest and diligent application of a creative and finely tuned programme of action can save Nigeria, nay, Africa and the Third World, from an inevitable slide into social and political morass and of course the severest economic and political irruption. No demagogic formula, no amount of sloganeering, no wishful thinking, and no repertory of decrees can reverse this trend or position.

We have to recognize the fact that the wealth of a nation does not consist in money, but in the goods that men use and their skill in getting or making them. The glib talk and allusions one hears so often these days about the exchange rate of the naira, or its revaluation should give way to serious theories of political economy and the recognition of the fact that the value of a nation's currency is inextricably tied to the productivity of the economy. Indeed, the fact about revolution in our living standard in Nigeria is that it would either come now through the Socratic Method of questioning and creative praxis or else through a bloody civil commotion and pillage. The choice is ours to make. And the time to make that choice is at hand.

Our inclination is towards the first option; that is, in the reconstruction of the Nigerian state and economy through Socratic questioning and creativity. And the idea we put forward today is a humble attempt at producing such an enabling philosophy. The proposal we are about to present inthe next chapter sets out to provide novel fiscal policy measures, appropriate for our time and circumstance that should boost the economy and make the society more vibrant and humane. At the risk of sounding impetuous and opinionated, we proclaim that through the application of the ideas or recommendations here enunciated, our social and economic circumstance will certainly be redressed and made more wholesome.

CHAPTER 4

RECIPE FOR NATIONAL ECONOMIC AND SOCIAL DEVELOPMENT

The economic recovery programme which Nigeria has adopted in the last four decades is based on the analysis of our problems made by the World Bank and the International Monetary Fund (IMF). According to that analysis, the reason for our economic difficulties is the strangulation of government bureaucracy on the freedom of economic action of the people. Corruption, mistaken policy options, the misdirection of economic efforts, and even political instability are seen as the by-products of the pervasive excesses of state power. Accordingly, it is suggested that we would overcome our difficulties only if government takes its hands off all economic activities and sells all its investments to individuals who will work in cooperation and competition with each other.

All banks, breweries, airways, shipping lines, petroleum wells and refineries, electricity generating stations, telecommunication services, etc. owned by government must be sold to private investors. At the same time no licence should be needed for any imports. Nor should the international value of the naira be subject to regulation. International trade should be liberalized to allow a free flow of goods and services around the world. In the same way, banking deposits and loans should be made in a freely competitive manner, without undue restrictions from monetary authorities.

The general idea is that the release of the creative freedom of individuals, each person exploiting opportunities for profit in an open market, would create a more vibrant national economy than any plan made by stuffy bureaucracy. This policy direction was christened Structural Adjustment Programme, SAP. So far most of the cardinal policy prescriptions of SAP have been enacted and put into operation. The Privatisation programme, the highpoint of SAP, has virtually been completed. Even so, Nigeria has very little to show for its obedience and dedication to the World Bank/IMF and their policy direction.

Government's continued insistence on a national economic programme that is anchored almost entirely on privatisation, foreign investment and a tinkering with money supply can be faulted both from practical and theoretical standpoints. In almost all instances, privatisation has been followed by massive retrenchment of workers in the privatised enterprises as the new company managements prune the staffing in these companies to make for 'efficiency' and profitability. The general tendency has been a resort to hi-tech equipment, which generally displace human labour at the workplace. In effect, deregulation and privatisation have encouraged technological unemployment. But because the Nigerian private sector is itself too weak and ill-equipped to absorb the laid-off former public servants, the unemployment situation in the country has worsened, indeed skyrocketed, with its attendant negative social consequences.

Secondly, SAP does not possess an intrinsic mechanism for managing the debilitating impact of the massive inflation that has accompanied its liberalization policy. Thus, acting in concert with other forces of the market place, the hyperinflation generated under SAP has led to a progressive fall in the aggregate disposable income of the masses. This has reduced the purchasing power of those whose incomes are adversely affected by inflationary pressure, leading, as we shall see later in this text, to dire consequences for the economy.

Thirdly, the impact of SAP on economic growth has not been appreciable. The expected boom in domestic non-oil production expected to accompany the introduction of the Structural Adjustment Programme has not come about. The much-vaunted hope that the drastic reduction in the quantum of imported goods in the early years of the introduction of the programme and its devaluation content would encourage economic agents in the productive sector to produce more, has not really materialised. This goes to prove that the mere co-existence of scarcity (of needed goods) with an abundance of unemployed but employable human labour and even of investment capital, cannot by themselves generate a burst in investment and production in a depressed economy. They usually await an enabling and generative economic policy to ignite and translate that potentiality into a heightened level of economic activity. This generative punch is what really is lacking in SAP. And this is why it has not made the requisite impact even after the privatisation of the remaining government parastatals.

So, from whichever direction one looks at it, our continued reliance on SAP as the vehicle for national economic reconstruction, recovery and progress is fraught with danger. Its dismal performance and ineffectiveness, even after the virtual completion of privatization, with respect to the three vital macro-economic indices of Employment, Inflation and Growth spell doom for the nation and the economy.

Oh yes, we agree that privatisation has brought a measure of efficiency in the service sector, in power supply, telecommunications, etc. But its overall impact on the real sector, in manufacturing, agriculture, etc., remains, as experience has shown, somewhat ineffectual, if not downright negative. The inflationary pressure in the system persists as the value of the national currency continues to plummet in the light of the weak productive base of the economy.

The unemployment situation has worsened as more and more people are thrown off work with the privatisation of the remaining government parastatals and equities in companies. It is even possible that with the last government's liberalisation policy on imports and fall of oil prices, Nigeria might run into a balance-of-payments disequilibrium of the kind that hit the country in the dying days of the Second Republic - a development that will definitely compound an already complicated situation on ground. Trade arrears will mount and Nigeria will risk isolation again from the international market place.

Indeed, our experience in Nigeria so far is that the deepening of privatization and commercialization programmes and the so-called free-market economic policies recommended by the IMF and the World Bank have led to concentration of wealth in fewer and fewer hands.

It is the view of the IMF and the World Bank that apart from implementing the cardinal policies of SAP like privatization, the Central Bank of Nigeria (CBN) should engage in a periodic mop up of excess liquidity of money in circulation in order to curtail demand for foreign exchange, curb the recessionary pressure in the system and so revitalize economic activities.

Balanced budgets are also recommended to complement the above. In adopting this posture, they are basically following Milton Friedman, the Chief of the monetary school of economics, who on the basis of discovering that a correlation exists between changes in money supply and changes in the level of business activity, goes ahead to claim that fluctuations in money supply cause fluctuations in national income.

In other words, that the periodic economic cycle of boom, recession, depression and recovery, is to be attributed entirely to changes in money supply. (Monetarists claim that the severity of the Great Depression of the 1930s was due to a major contraction of money supply, citing the fact that money supply declined by 35 per cent between 1929 and 1933 in the United States). This monetarist approach of the IMF and World Bank seems to discard in its entirety the valid testimony of an equally influential school of economic thought, the neo-Keynesians, who maintain that control of money supply is not the most important factor in combating recessions and depressions.

Are we then suggesting that government should resort to neo-Keynesian remedies, by pumping direct investment into the economy, say through erecting industrial plants across the country, to provide work, employment and growth for the people and the economy respectively? Or should Government find some other ways of directly providing work for the army of the unemployed in the land?

Not necessarily. The level of financial and managerial indiscipline in the system alone is enough to stifle such effort.

Actually, we are not against privatisation per se. However, we endorse the neo-Keynesian viewpoint that monetary policy alone cannot grapple with major depressions; that government intervention is necessary when the economy shows signs of settling down to a period of stable but high unemployment, as is now the case with the Nigerian economy. We agree that it is dangerous, wrong and defeatist to leave the problem to natural or market forces. Lord Keynes was right when he argued in his theory of Underemployment Equilibrium that there is a possibility of permanent (or at least long-lived) depression in the absence of government intervention, because although natural or market forces usually act to move an economy from a depression or unemployment position back to full employment, these forces act so slowly that they can be discountenanced for all practical purposes.

Indeed, CBN's periodic liquidity mop-up operations do not inspire hope and optimism that the use of that instrument will reverse the recession/depression we experience so very often and restore vibrancy to the economy. So far what these liquidity mop-ups have done is to push interest (lending) rates through the roof. With the mop-ups, players in the nation's foreign exchange market are forced to source naira at more and more cost leading to high interest rates. With an economy running at over 25 per cent interest rate, it is obvious that no sane investor will borrow to start new industrial plants or manufacturing processes. For at such an interest rate the business will be crippled even before take- off; before the erection of the plant is completed.

Conversely, what we have today is that virtually all bank lending largely goes to finance import trade in Nigeria, for it is only such short-time borrowers that can bear the extremely high cost of money in Nigeria. Today, therefore what we have is an import-trade economy. All kinds of cheap imports flood the country discouraging local production and indeed asphyxiating local industry and manufacturing. Consequently, many Nigerian youths who should be factory/farm-hands are displaced from the workplace and are forced to take to all forms of hassles in the name of business, trade and employment, while others take to crime.

We tend to overlook the fact that although orthodox monetary and fiscal policies make reasonable impact on the workings of the advanced industrial economies, the local environment places strong limitations on their effectiveness here. The reasons are quite obvious.

Apart from the fact that the level of financial and managerial indiscipline in the country is too high, one has to contend with the prevalence of weak socio-economic structures and institutional imperfections and peculiarities of a developing country like Nigeria. What quantity of currency in circulation is within the banking system? What is the size of Nigerian's banking public? How efficient and how strong is the Nigerian Capital Market?

Ours is largely an informal economy where cash transactions predominate. This keeps most of the money in circulation outside the banking system. The other factor that encourages people to keep their money outside the banking system is the fact that interest rates on deposits are very low even when lending rates are so very high. The informal nature of the economy also keeps most businesses outside the purview of government taxation.

These are some of the reasons why orthodox monetary and fiscal instruments employed in advanced economies - discount rate adjustments, variable reserve requirements, open-market operations, etc. - make little impact on the Nigerian economy, as in some other Third World economies. The relative ineffectiveness or, indeed, failure of these orthodox policies over the decades has become a source of worry and consternation in many circles and has made many Nigerians believe, as they put it, that the Nigerian economy does not obey the laws of economics.

It is perhaps pertinent at this stage to reflect on governments' attempts in the past few years to reflate the economy via the award of multi-billion naira contracts for all manner of public works – road construction and rehabilitation, power stations, dams, etc. The idea of reflating the economy presupposes that the award of these contracts would through a trickle-down effect enhance the purchasing power of the average Nigerian and hence effect increases in consumption demand, which in turn, would have a salutary effect on production. But the reality is that all these hopes have been dashed. Despite increased government expenditure on construction, there is practically no positive effect on productivity. The purchasing power of the masses of Nigerians remains low. Indeed, there is no trickle-down effect to write home about. What then should we attribute this failure to?

It is one of the peculiarities of developing countries that foreign companies and multinationals dominate the bulk of their construction industry. Nigeria is no exception to this rule. The bulk of the nation's construction works are awarded to multinationals. But these companies tend to rely more on high-tech equipment in the execution of their contracts. There is a general de-emphasis of labour-intensive approach in the execution of the works. It is not unusual for instance, to see earth-movers and other such contraption digging trenches and gutters while jobless labourers standby or roam the streets without work.

Secondly, because of the glut in manpower resources in the country, road-building and general contractors in Nigeria, multinational as well as local ones, pay low wages to their labourers. The cumulative effect is that a very little portion of the huge contract sums paid out by government for these public works actually get to the labourers and the mass of the nation's unemployed artisans and trained construction workers.

It is our expectation that even the recent calls for government to grant tax-cuts and rebates to companies as a way of reflating the economy will not fare much better. It will not, given the structure of the Nigerian economy, lead to any appreciable increase in the purchasing power of majority of Nigerians. Its impact will hardly reach the masses or better their disposable incomes. Indeed, no appreciable reflation of the economy will be achieved through the advocated tax cuts and rebates for the same reasons that were adduced in the case of construction contracts.

The point in all this is that the over-reliance on orthodox monetary and fiscal policy instruments in the management and control of a Third World economy like ours is inherently counter-productive. This argument is made against the backdrop of the prevalence of weak socio-economic structures in Third World economies and the poor degree to which real magnitudes in such economies respond to orthodox or traditional monetary/fiscal policies. Secondly, it is observed that institutional imperfections and peculiarities of developing countries limit the effectiveness of monetary and credit instruments. Consequently, because these policies do not exercise the appropriate influence on productive activities, they cannot exert the appropriate influence on income and the overall health of the Nigerian economy.

The bottom line is that the peculiarities of our circumstance and the goals we aim at necessitate the introduction of new and extraordinary measures to direct and improve the performance of the Nigerian economy. The orthodox traditional system espoused by the World Bank, the IMF and their agents will not do. In fact, they have failed!

Privatization, liberalization, devaluation, control of money supply, etc. may in the long-term help in the overall task of restoring economic buoyancy in Nigeria, but they cannot by themselves accomplish that goal, nor do they represent the most important instruments in the achievement of that result. If we continue to rely on these instruments, which have already failed us anyway, without reaching for certain crucial adjustments, the country's economic problems will worsen.

The deepening economic crisis will rub off on social order and harmony. There will be more beggars on the streets, an army of destitute and more crime. Above all, because of the huge social dislocation and tension that would follow, a startling paradox might come into focus: Government might be tempted, in fact, compelled to invade every facet of society in order to enforce social cohesion, to whip everybody into line. For a leap into the Hobbesian jungle of economic deregulation readily leads to political regulation. Pinochet's

Chile, where Friedman's theories were particularly first tried out, is a case in point.

Furthermore, government's forlorn hope of attracting foreign investment and indeed, of making it a cornerstone of its economic revitalization policy is palpable. Foreign investment on the scale contemplated by government cannot go hand in hand with tough capital controls, in view of the low international confidence in our economy. Before the big foreign investors can venture into these parts, they would demand conditions and safeguards that would test any government and indeed make it subordinate, in practical terms, to the whims of the foreign investors. They would, for instance, demand an open-door policy with respect to movement of capital to and from the country. Under such a climate, capital flight from the country will get out of hand. Reference is made here to Dr Nnamdi Azikiwe's *Liberia in World Politics* (1929).

Secondly, we might have an influx of 'hot money' from global portfolio investors or stock market players with the hot tip, who are ever ready to rush out, capital in tow, at the slightest hint of trouble. Given the unstable nature of our polity, this arrangement will, in the short to medium term, put the economy into a new kind of stress and instability. It could precipitate a Mexico-type (December 1994) economic collapse in which a spurt of unexpected capital flight led to a peso crash, revealing that nation's open market excesses and inherent danger in relying on foreign capital and investment as a primary factor in Third World development strategy.

The lesson in all this is that we do not have to expose our soft under-belly to the international stock-players: that it is patently wrong to predicate the country's economic advancement on a factor that is quite outside the control of Nigerians and that does not make development people-oriented.

A viable economic programme must be inward-looking, relying on the resources (financial and otherwise) immediately available to us. The infusion of foreign capital and investment into the country must not be taken for granted or considered crucial to our survival and development. No doubt, we must create a favourable climate for the attraction of foreign investment, but this external component of our development strategy must be seen only as supplementary to our efforts. They must not subsume the latter. Our attitude should be such that if foreign investment comes, we accept it; if it doesn't, we still forge ahead and get on with the task at hand.

The government must adopt fresh ideas and development strategy as well as enforce the financial and managerial discipline we need to get the economy moving. To survive as a people, we need to create conditions for increased investment in every sector of the economy; turn the emphasis from importation of finished goods to local production; check the adverse effects of inflation on the economy; curtail or reduce the current high interest rate in the system; solve the problem of unemployment; encourage the development of local technology; and of course ensure that the rural communities have the productive base to give us food security and provide raw materials for our industries. It should be our resolve to promote the adoption of the above goals by the new civilian administration and to provide a concrete and workable format for the achievement of these goals.

After thorough study and analysis, we think we can put forward a strategy that is bound to ensure the realisation of the above goals. We believe that within the short run the application of the measures we envisage would reverse the persistent recession/depression syndrome presently afflicting the nation and put the economy on the road to recovery and boom. Tall and difficult as this task might appear, it can indeed be accomplished through the application of a seemingly simple and innocuous strategy.

To appreciate the efficacy of this strategy, one first has to understand the underlying factors responsible for the economic recession and depression that have been the lot of the Nigerian economy in the last four decades, and in fact, the major forces at play in the periodic cycle of recession, depression, recovery and boom that is so prevalent in modern economies.

Summing Up

To recap, the Nigerian society and economy like many other nations and economies around the world are afflicted by the following;

1. A general propensity on the part of employers and company managers to appropriate disproportionately high percentages of company incomes or added value to themselves;

2. Government's inability to moderate the above situation through its stipulation of minimum wage;

3. The consequent low purchasing power of the masses lowers consumption which leads to low

sales by producers, and ultimately recession/depression.

From the foregoing, it is clear that we subscribe to the generally accepted notion that low purchasing power of consumers has been a crucial factor in the sustenance of the long period of economic depression in Nigeria. That a lowered aggregate purchasing power of consumers inevitably leads to low sales on the part of producers and manufacturers. As sales dwindle, producers are generally forced to lower production or risk having their warehouses filled with unsold and overflowing inventory.

Of course when these changes begin to occur, they are fuelled by expectations which during a recession could cause further deceleration of the economy. A cumulative and significant cutback on production then necessitates a reduction of workforce or retrenchment of workers by producers and manufacturers and, by extension, companies in the service industry.

This demoralising scenario is actually tantamount to a recession. As more and more workers are retrenched and the unemployment situation worsens, so is the aggregate purchasing power of consumers further dampened; since more and more people are now forced to go without incomes. The end result of this trend is a depression, which could get prolonged if the right antidotes are not employed and applied to reverse the ugly situation.

By implication, the right antidote to the situation must be such that puts more money into the hands of the average person or the masses of workers in the country, such that aggregate purchasing power is enhanced. Improved purchasing power would of course enhance consumption demand, increase sales and make producers to produce more, employ more workers and indeed increase investment in the economy. This is what economists generally refer to as Recovery. Sustenance of such positive trend inevitably leads to a Boom, the fourth stage in the periodic cyclic changes that characterise modern economies.

In recent times, the Nigerian Federal Government has applied a number of measures with which it hoped to put more money in the hands of the average person or to reflate the economy as the jargon goes. But most of these measures, as already discussed, have ended up unmitigated failures. The only aspect of government's measure that has made some remarkable impact in the drive to reflate the economy is the general increase in the salaries of workers in the public sector of the nation's economy. By stipulating a new enhanced minimum wage for workers and indeed implementing a new and better salary structure in the public sector, government workers have been put in a good position to consume more, although the salutary impact of the above on the economy has been dampened by an import dependency syndrome which takes business away from local producers and manufacturers.

However, the bulk of the nation's workforce which is outside the public sector, which makes up the nation's private sector, has not really been touched by the legislation on minimum wage, or the general and significant increases in salaries and wages. The reasons are easy to discern. In the first place, that legislation is unenforceable in the private sector of the economy where incomes vary widely from onesub-sector to another, and from company to company. There is no doubt that some companies, by virtue of their low incomes, cannot pay the minimum wages stipulated or canvassed by government. Yet there are companies who are in a position to pay more than two to ten times the minimum wage proposed by government but would not do so without a push, for obvious reasons.

In the Western World where giant and powerful trade unionism thrives, it might be possible or easy (though doubtful in view of current developments) for such trade unions to compel capable and potentially strong companies to increase salaries and wages and so help drag the economy out of a recession or depression by virtue of the enhanced purchasing power of consumers that would accompany such wage increases. But it is part of the weak socioeconomic structures and institutional imperfections and peculiarity of the Nigerian nation that there are no strong trade unions to play such a role in the country. Thus, the last category of companies mentioned in the last paragraph who have the way and means to sustain higher wages and indeed to substantially increase the earnings of their workers, but would not do so, are allowed to get away with such inimical practice, even as incomes per man-hour dangerously outstrip pay per man-hour in such companies.

It will be recalled, courtesy *Time Magazine* (Feb. 1,1982) that a prevailing view as to what caused the Great Depression of the 1930s, as persuasively argued by John Kenneth Galbraith, is that the technological increases in productivity throughout the 1920s (up 43% per factory man- hour) were not matched by increases in wages and thus in the public's capacity to consume (factory pay rose less than 20%).

The fact that the former did not match the latter meant that the public's capacity to buy finished goods and services fell, leading to a stockpile of unsold inventory in factory warehouses across America. The attempt to cut back on production in order to forestall further accumulation of unsold goods brought about massive retrenchments which in turn further lowered aggregate disposable incomes and the public's capacity to consume or buy goods. It was this persistent and cumulative fall in consumption demand that produced a recession that eventually led to the severe Great Depression of the 1930s.

In Nigeria it must be noted, researchers at the Nigerian Institute of Social and Economic Research (NISER) have shown that the percentage of national income appropriated by Nigerian workers rose from 27.69% in 1973/74 to 32% in 1975/76, as a result of the Udoji salary increases. The Udoji Award caused the frenzy in economic activities witnessed in the year 1975/6. From this height, the percentage of national income appropriated by workers (also known as employee compensation) fell steadily dropping to about 21% in 1985/86, at the start of the Structural Adjustment Programme. (See Table 1)

TABLE 1.

Employees Compensation in Nigeria

Year	Compensation (%)
1973/74*	27.6
1975/76*	32.0
1981	22.81
1982	23.10
1983	23.13
1984	21.68
1985	21.03
1986	21.71

Calculated from data of Federal Office of Statistics (FOS)

* From African Development Bank (ADB) sources. [See also Nwankwo, Uchenna, *Economic Agenda for Nigeria* (1992) p. 247]

It is also estimated that by 1992, labour share of national income had fallen further to about 13%. Indeed, these declines have been productive of a massively lowered aggregate purchasing power of the masses of Nigerian people as well as a persistent massive recessionary pressure on the economy, just as the peak in aggregate disposable income created by Udoji Award caused the frenzy or boom in economic activities recorded in the mid-seventies.

The problem in Nigeria, as in many other countries of the world, therefore is that for as long as incomes remain depressed in the private sector especially, for so long will purchasing power of the generality of Nigerian consumers remain low, to the detriment of the economy. The question therefore remains: what steps should we take to enhance the take-home pay in the Nigerian private sector in order to enhance aggregate purchasing power of consumers, increase consumption demand, ensure that the new consumption pattern would enhance production of local goods and services, and so stimulate local manufacturing and industry, as well as improve local technology and curb indiscipline and corruption in the system?

Universality of the Problem

Of course the phenomenon of perennial depreciation of labour share of national income is not peculiar to Nigeria. It is more or less universal. We have made reference to the notion that "what caused the Great Depression of the 1930s in the Western World or US in particular, as persuasively argued by John Kenneth Galbraith, is that the technological increases in productivity throughout the 1920s (up 43% per factory man-hour) were not matched by increases in wages and thus in the public's capacity to consume (factory pay rose less than 20%)." This supports the viewpoint of the phenomenon of stagnated or depressing labour share of national incomes in the Western world then.

A more recent study of the phenomenon from the Economic Policy Institute of the United States of America shows that: whereas productivity in that country rose by nearly 74% for the period 1973 to 2016, wages rose only by 12.5%. This means that the value-added in industry were increasingly appropriated by owners of capital while labour price actually stagnated or rose marginally in recent times. (See Chart I below)

Similarly, the management cadre and senior staff of companies appropriate disproportionate sizes of the income due the Labour force thereby short-changing the people at the lower rung of the salary scale, especially the segment at the very bottom of the income scale. In the latest analysis of CEO pay, the US Economic Policy Institute (EPI) states that the pay of Chief Executive Officers (CEO) have grown by 940% since 1978, while typical workers' pay grew only 12% during the same time. According to the analysis, CEOs were paid an average of $17.2 million in 2018, which is 278 times what typical workers were paid. It goes on to state that extraordinarily high CEO pay is not a reflection of increased productivity or high-demand skills but of CEOs' power to set their own pay – and is a major contributor to rising inequality. See Chart III for illustrations.

Source: Economic Policy Institute, US

It is all about the disconnection between wages and productivity in modern American workplace. The sad fact is that real wages have declined for most Americans despite huge gains in productivity over the last several decades. As it is in the Western world, so it is in Nigeria. The only difference is in the way citizens or the working class in the two worlds react to the subsisting syndrome. While Nigerians adopt corrupt methods of augmenting their respective wages, in the United States the working class are inclined to living on bank loans and all manner of hire purchases to make ends meet. As a consequence, the American working class now generally live and die as debtors, with their total consumer debts and hire purchases running into about 13 trillion dollars.

The rising inequality in the US is already worse than the 1929 situation, at the arrival of the Great Depression. (See Chart II) The share of wealth of the richest 10% of the US families in 2013 was 76% of the total wealth while the bottom 50% of families held 1%. This marks the highest level of concentration of wealth in the US since the 1930s.

The rising inequality of the present age is already threatening the social and economic system, and is now taking a political colouration and dimension as the rising army of angry poor American working class turn towards socialism and neo-Fascism as panacea for their biting economic conditions which worsen by the day.

Similarly, the number of Americans living on the dole is rising while some others increasingly call for higher taxation for the wealthy. Indeed, the consequences of these developments on America's future promise to be very impactful.

Holdings of Family Wealth

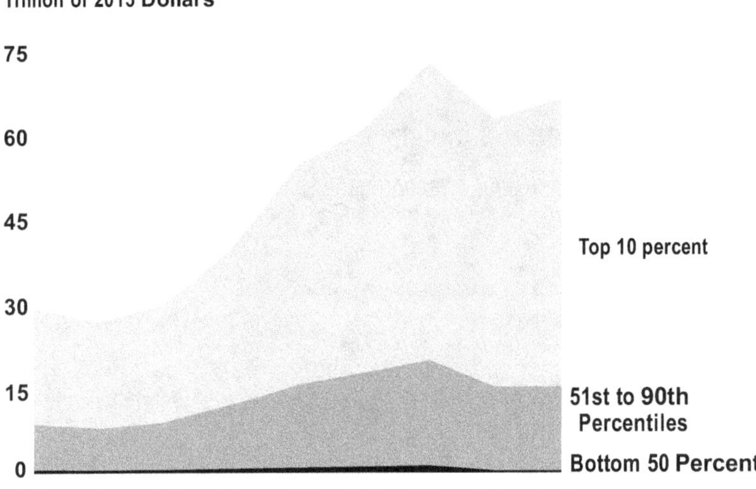

CBO Chart, U.S. Holdings of Family Wealth 1989 to 2013. The top 10% of families held 76% of the wealth in 2013, while the bottom 50% of families held 1%. Inequality worsened from 1989 to 2013.

Wealth inequality in the United States (also known as the **wealth gap**) is the unequal distribution of assets among residents of the United States. Wealth includes the values of homes, automobiles, personal valuables, businesses, savings, and investments. The net worth of U.S. households and non-profit organizations was $94.7 trillion in the first quarter of 2017, a record level both in nominal terms and purchasing power parity. If divided equally among 124 million U.S. households, this would be $760,000 per family; however, the bottom 50% of families, representing 62 million American households, average $11,000 net worth. From an international perspective, the difference in US median and mean wealth per adult is over 600%.

Chart III

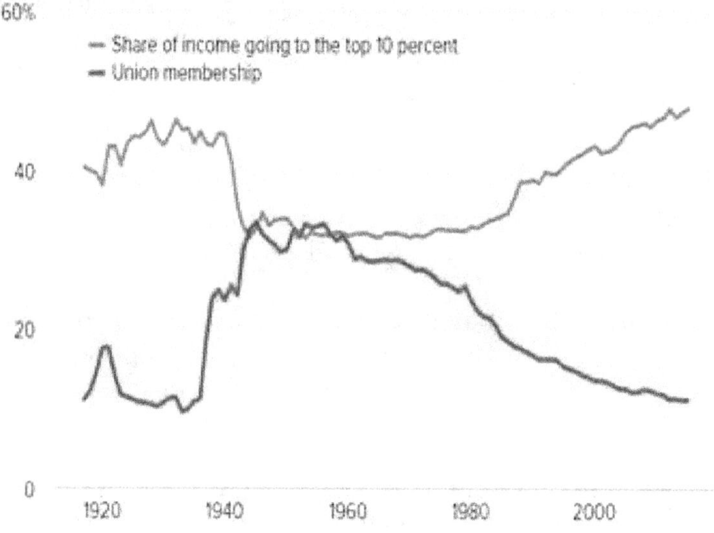

Source: Economic Policy Institute, US

Policy Prescription

In the light of the above observations and developments, we ask again, what must be done to stave off the looming implosion and cataclysm that are bound to accompany deteriorating socioeconomic conditions in Nigeria and elsewhere?

We seek the answers from the *centrist* ideology, which by this thesis must be at once socialistic and capitalistic. In other words, it must preserve the market system with its ingrained competition while at the same time encouraging mass or general involvement of the people in critical decision-making processes even at the micro-level or the level of companies as well as ensure that there is equity and fair distribution of the fruits of industry between Capital and Labour in business organisations: ditto between the managerial class or the management cadre and senior staff of companies and the lower class of labourers in the workplace. In this regard, we make the following prescriptions;

1. Government must ensure that Labour-share of national income is optimised (at all times) by stipulating that labour-share of company income or added-value shall not fall below a given minimum level or percentage for all business enterprises operating in the country.

2. It should also be stipulated that within a company, the total emolument, including allowances, of the highest paid worker, the managing director or CEO,

must not be more than twenty times that of the lowest paid worker.

3. Government must immediately institute a process of direct taxation of company income or added-value as against the present system of taxing company profit.

These three steps should constitute the major policy-instruments in the struggle to anchor the centrist ideology with respect to socio-economic matters as well as to stimulate the economy and put it on the path of sustainable growth and development. They should also help improve local technology, curb indiscipline and corruption, etc.

Other minor or traditional policy instruments to complement the above (in Nigeria) shall constitute in;

(a) The application of the principle of differential sectorial taxation, by which investment in critically depressed but vital sectors of the economy, like Agriculture, is to be encouraged by the offer of special enhanced tax incentives for companies operating in the given sector(s). (This should enhance profitability and help channel more investment into such sectors);

(b) The intensification of infrastructural development and maintenance of existing public utilities. (This should include the construction of an East/West standard-gauge rail-line running from Calabar to Lagos and another South/North rail-line running from Warri to Abuja: ditto the reconstruction of the rail-lines running from PH and Lagos to the North. The implementation of this policy will not only help create a needed initial spurt of employment of the magnitude that would help invigorate the economy but will equally enhance speedy, safe transportation of goods and the mass movement of people around the country. It will equally curtail or drastically reduce the huge foreign exchange and other resources annually channelled into the importation and deployment of motor-vehicles and spare parts in the country.)

(c) The use of available monetary and fiscal instruments to drastically reduce importation of foreign goods into the country and indeed provide necessary protection for local industry, as well as bring down interest rates (lending) while boosting interest rates paid by banks on bank deposits. In this regard, the CBN should stipulate that lending rates should not exceed $(x + 10)$ per cent for now, where x is equal to the prevailing rate of interest for deposit money.

(d) Steady and periodic review of salaries in the public sector to attune same to developments in the private sector must be implemented as a way of enhancing productivity, boosting morale and reducing corrupt practices in the sector.

(e) Enactment and enforcement of stiff penalties against future perpetrators of corruption in the land.

(f) Government is to stipulate a minimum number of professional staff for consultancy firms that handle government projects. This should differ for each professional group and should be related to the absolute number of qualified professionals within respective professional groups.

CHAPTER 5

EFFICACY OF THE RECOMMENDATION

Having outlined the above policy-measures, let us now go into the nitty-gritty of how the three major policy instruments above would impact on the set objectives.

As an overview, let us say that it is obvious that a policy of enhancing and stabilizing labour share of company (national) income will have a direct salutary impact expected from the general increase of consumer purchasing power that it will ensure. Such salutary impact would be further enhanced when viewed at the national scale. This spread effect is bound to lead to a more enhanced normal distribution of national income. It will bring more and more people towards the centre or mean of the income spectrum, broadening the base of the middle class to produce or reshape society for the better.

With a fairer distribution of incomes, aggregate disposable incomes will be enhanced. This means that with the introduction of this policy, there shall be a steady upward movement in consumption demand. Companies, manufacturers and producers in general shall begin to record more sales. Conversely, they shall begin to increase production, employ more workers and retool.

In other words, the economic stagnation that has been with us for decades will begin to ebb and some upsurge in economic activity shall come into evidence. But above that, certain intrinsic changes shall occur over our attenuating economic behaviour and attitudes and impact positively on our economic life and the way things are hitherto shaped.

Such changes shall be felt in the area of:

1). Modes of production employed in industry;
2). Choices of technology in manufacturing
    and industrial production;
3). The general level of employment;
4). The general impact of inflation;
5). Crime wave;
6). The trend towards big government; and
7). Financial discipline at the work place, among others.

These points require further elucidation.

The direct and immediate consequence of the increased consumer purchasing power envisaged at the introduction of the above policies, we have agreed, is rising consumption demand, sales and productivity. This means that there will be an upswing in installed capacity utilization in many of our industries, manufacturing plants and agricultural establishments.

For the investor who would want to take advantage of the general increase in consumption demand to introduce new products or services, establish a new factory, farm or expand an existing one, the immediate impact of the policy would be a reappraisal of production technique he contemplates to employ. Being mindful of the fact that under the new dispensation, he would be obliged to allocate nothing less than a given minimum percentage of company income (value-added) to labour and labour matters, notwithstanding the size of the company's fixed capital assets, he would definitely elect to employ a more labour- intensive method of production than present situation and conditions demand. It will be foolhardy and cost ineffective, both in terms of capital input and return on investment, to do otherwise.

By this token, companies would be able to optimize the use of human labour at the work-place, thereby curtailing the negative impact of technological unemployment which is poised to gain the upper-hand under the prevailing conditions in the country. It is indeed sickening to watch, for instance, road construction companies use complicated machines to dig gutters or drains while countless unemployed labourers loiter about wondering where their next meal would come from.

Furthermore, the preponderance of labour-intensive production methods, especially in the manufacturing and service sectors, would reduce the importation of certain foreign highly automated or hi-tech systems and shift emphasis to simpler, appropriate technologies, which we can, with little effort, develop and maintain locally. Our scientists and engineers will thus be able to adapt, design and build moderate-sized oil refineries, cement plants and other manufacturing outfits, which they can run and maintain even as their counterparts in the defunct Biafran enclave did.

This would save the country from sinking deeper and deeper into the susceptibility of subtle blackmail by which we are perennially compelled to periodically spend unexpected fantastic fortunes on so-called turn-around maintenance of complicated foreign-built refineries, cement and steel plants, and other advanced technologies we can ill- afford. We shall then be able to start small, build small and advance layer after layer, knowing that we shall have grasp of a qualitative and sustainable technological culture in the end, rather than continue to wallow in the present, stifling, century-old system of aping the whites, trying to build skyscrapers on quicksand and without solid foundation. This can be likened to the Japanese, Indian and Chinese approach to technological development that was based on a stringent inward-looking strategy which has succeeded even beyond the dreams of the architects of that tradition.

In sum, rising capacity utilization in existing industries, increased and general adoption of appropriate technologies and labour-intensive production techniques induced by the principal policy thrust above would combine to combat unemployment in a decisive way. The overall picture is that a massive employment drive by different companies, old as well as new, in both the service and productive sectors, will ensue. As the general level of employment in the country rises, so shall aggregate purchasing power and the public's demand for goods and services. With rising demand and sales, there would be increased investment and productivity.

Predictably, the initial burst of economic activity shall be felt in the agricultural sector given its low entry requirement and adaptability to labour-intensive modes of production. These prospects shall be further enhanced with the exportation of certain local food products because the move would help create the price-incentive that should ensure further investment in agriculture and its allied industries.

Furthermore, since the main consequences of inflation is to redistribute income among people, benefiting those who earn their income through commissions, rents, profits, etc., and hurting wage-earners, the policy of linking factor-shares to company income or added-value goes a long way in ameliorating this negative unfair consequence of inflation.

We also expect that a direct consequence of the expanding prosperity, rising employment and general economic well-being painted above will be felt in the social sector. There is no gainsaying the fact that the deepening national economic crisis we have faced in the last four or so decades have rubbed off on social order and harmony. There are more beggars in the streets, an army of destitute and more crime. Against the backdrop that human behaviour is dependent on both innate and environmental characteristics, the promise of prosperity and job creation offered above is bound to reverse the ugly trend and restore hope in the nation, as well as faith, trust and overall civility in interpersonal relationships.

Furthermore, under the new dispensation, the creeping threat of big government, under which many newer prisons are being planned for the country, will be dampened. As the present level of crime subsides, so shall the cost and attempt by government to police everybody and everything, as well as administer a mammoth welfare programme that could fuel corruption. It is particularly startling that Nigeria has degenerated to a level where the military and virtually every other national security apparatus have become functional agencies for internal social control and crime fighting – a role, we all know, that is quite outside their constitutional role of warding off external aggression and checking political insurrection.

Impact on Financial Indiscipline at the Workplace

Finally, there is the problem of financial indiscipline at the workplace, of corruption in high and low places. Needless to say, this constitutes one of the biggest obstacles to national development, justice and fairness everywhere. How, you would ask, will a credible government tackle this social and national malady? To address this issue, one has to ask himself why corruption has remained so pervasive and intractable in the society.

It is our considered opinion that some of the factors that have fuelled corruption, social decadence and national degeneracy are:

Absence of democracy;
A relative lack of competition in work and industry; andLack of openness in the management of group affairs.

Former Soviet leader, Mikhail Gorbachev, put his finger on this point when he talked of *Perestroika* and *Glasnost*. We use the term lack of democracy here to denote an absence of political pluralism within a society. And we posit that the presence of strong, legal and responsive opposition parties or party constitutes one of the most effective methods of checking the excesses of a ruling party and a reminder to a corruptive regime that it could be thrown out of office unless it mended its ways. Where there is no legal opposition, the ruling clique generally degenerates into a merry gang whose focus, aspirations and pursuits become quite abstracted from those of the people they lead, resulting in decay, corruption and other dire consequences. Didn't the old adage posit that absolute power corrupts absolutely?

The fate of the defunct Soviet Union and many other totalitarian and dictatorial states and regimes are cases in point. Therefore, that Nigeria has democracy today, however fragile it is at the moment, is something we must cherish and try to make more wholesome. We must take every measure necessary to restore and preserve democracy, the political rights of every individual, group or party as a partial and abiding method of checking corruption, graft and recklessness in high places, and for the overall good of our people. Similarly, strong trade unionism and authentic leaderships of the unions must be guaranteed and given teeth to encourage the practice of collective bargaining and the overall welfare of the nation's workforce.

Of course competition and competitiveness are part and parcel of the democratic tradition. But they do transcend politics and the natural rivalries inherent in governance and public affairs. Their frontiers encompass business and other economic relations. In the old socialist order, where production ceilings, qualities, and techniques of production in industry, including the variety and prices of goods and services produced were all virtually centrally planned and determined, competition between production units or companies is severely curtailed, leading once again to wrong priorities, shortages, hoarding and corruption.

Fortunately, competition is relatively guaranteed in this society via the market system. Of course there is still room for improvement, as there may be areas where past and present governments may have inadvertently foisted in-competitiveness. It should be the priority of government to explore avenues to inculcate healthy competition in all aspects of our national life because the absence of these detract from the centrist ideology and exert very negative consequences on society.

Having examined the impact of the twin issues of democracy and competitiveness, let us now turn attention to the third factor, openness. To put it very mildly, this is one area where even the market-oriented systems have not shown adequate responsiveness. It is our opinion that when it comes to this subject of openness, especially at the micro- economic level, at the level of companies and business organizations, the system we operate has not gone far enough. There is little openness in the way these establishments are run. Consequently, this abiding and disruptive lack of openness, which holds sway, we have observed, largely at the company level shields much fraud, swindles of all kinds, tax evasion, etc. It is our contention that under certain conditions, the pollution and cover-ups perpetrated at these low places produce the rot which subsequently transcend and subsume the so-called high places, compromising government and quasi-public officials and reinforcing the form of decay and attrition that consign the nation to the vineyard of corruption and social paralysis.

Today in Nigeria, we can point to instances of total and enervating failure and corruption at the micro-level, at the level of companies or the private sector, which have produced darkling clouds that have enveloped the entire nation. We are aware that company owners and managers in Nigeria literally do and undo as they please. They fraudulently appropriate company resources, offer company funds as inducement and bribe to government officials and other external agencies. They keep two books or accounts: the real thing for themselves, and a doctored one for tax officials and other supervisory agencies.

Most of the external auditors or chartered accountants that are supposed to scrutinize company accounts largely function as mere rubber-stamps for legitimizing dubious company accounts and operations. It is no longer news that the (average) Nigerian corporate auditor has long abandoned any pretence to carrying out his statutory function in society. The continued reliance on this social category and their 'professional' judgment as the primary method of checking and of stemming frauds and embezzlements at the company level has long proven illusory and laughable. So, how do we begin to redress this situation and therefore return companies to the path of probity, accountability and openness, and by extension, checking their general corruptive influences in the society?

Let us first observe that we subscribe to the notion that given the degenerate status-quo, any plan to redress the situation on the ground must be all embracing and encompassing, providing every citizen with a role or roles to play in the prosecution of the above task. Nigeria has decidedly passed the time and stage where any social category, agency or functionaries of government, religious institutions, etc., acting alone or by themselves, even in concert, could hope to make any appreciable impact on the task of bringing the society back to restitution.

Moreover, anything that affects all must be tackled by all. To compel everybody to take adequate interest in the task, we must provide the necessary incentive. Thus at the workplace, at the micro-economic level, we have to make everybody, the shareholder, manager as the ordinary worker, a stakeholder in the enterprise.

We reckon that the policy of relating factor-shares and company taxation to company income or added-value enunciated above goes a long way in providing the requisite incentive, self-interest and openness that are called for. The system is bound to keep every member of a company or enterprise alert to the well-being of the organisation, to the need to plug avenues for leakage, plundering and waste in the system, as a way of maximizing profitability, factor shares and therefore individual take-home 'pay'.

Indeed, with labour share of company income made a percentage of company income, value-added or productivity, each worker would realise that the higher the value-added or income of the company the higher his 'pay'. Hence each worker would strive to help plug avenues for the depletion of that added-value as a means of shoring up his own personal share of that income.

It is our expectation that this attitudinal change, especially when expressed in macro-proportions, would in time rub off on the larger society and help instil the much-needed sanity and conformity at all levels, and anchor prudent norms and morality regarding correct and legitimate rules of behaviour in business. The labour unions shall wake up to the reality that they are not there to just canvass for fatter pay packets for workers but also to help check abuses, leakages and waste in the system. (The unions should actually have the right to carry out independent audits of company accounts since factor-shares are to be related to added-value of the company). This added responsibility will itself help strengthen labour unionism in the country and produce authentic and virile leaderships of the unions.

This would augur well with the society and economy because the presence of such structures as gleaned from the workings of Western industrial economies is direly needed here. Moreover, the presence of strong labour unionism should help consolidate the new culture of openness at the company level and enable underhanded deals to be laid bare and open to all interested parties. The policy will also help suck many more companies from the informal to the formal sector of the economy, thereby helping in the erection of reliable structures and the gathering of data on which economic planning and management may be predicated in the future.

Finally, let us reiterate that the attitude of our establishment economists and policy makers who act as if they are wedded to orthodox prescriptions and advance same as the only route through which the national economy could be salvaged do this nation a lot of harm. The Great Depression (1929 - 1939) in the United States had undermined faith in the orthodox philosophy of Laissez faire, according to which it was postulated that the disequilibrium of the market would eventually be restored to a new equilibrium without any interference from the outside. Roosevelt, though not an economist, had by practical exertion and principled benevolent action shown that such disequilibrium can be ameliorated without recourse to orthodox principles; in fact, that such policy orthodoxy is an impediment or, at best, ineffective in tackling a prolonged depression brought about by the collapse of economic Laissez faire.

Newsweek (Feb 1, 1982) captured the same scenario in the following words: "Roosevelt's New Deal was pragmatic rather than visionary, an improvisation of a practical order that you always get after a collapse." For 40 years the Nigerian economy has been, more or less, in recession / depression, or has been oscillating from recession/ depression to short-term recoveries because the crunch has finally come upon Nigeria's economic Laissez faire.

For those 40 years, many of our establishment economists have continued to express faith in the old order, in our moribund neo-laissez-faire economy, and to insist that the solution to the problem lies in the cornucopia of traditional orthodox remedies of the type continuously put forward by the 2010 visioning, the annual Economic Summits, etc. Our position is that those prescriptions are meretricious and not efficacious to development; that we must learn from the noble efforts of President Franklin Roosevelt and bring the crying economic woes of this country to an end by giving her a novel Fair Deal.

Common-sense dictates that we need to device an ideological format that is at once socialistic and individualistic; a format that combines the best attributes of the two great political ideologies: Socialism and Capitalism to produce what we now tag or label as the centrist ideology.

Background to the Scheme

Actually, the proposal put forward in the foregoing with respect to relations of production is not entirely new nor is the practice novel. Such practice is known to have had a long history – a history that predates the movement of individualism, which gave rise to the capitalist way of life. As a matter of fact, it implies for some of us a resuscitation of a system whose development and application was gradually terminated or diluted by the movement of individualism. It will be recalled that in the olden days, as in many surviving traditional societies, labour was never hired or employed for fixed salaries and wages. Instead labour-price or income used to be a definite customarily predetermined percentage of venture-income.

Examples of this practice may be found in records of ancient religions and history and in some existing traditional societies where this culture and practice have managed to survive the vicissitudes of time. Hence we find that in most cattle-rearing cultures, it is normal for the shepherd to be remunerated according to the number of off-springs produced by the flock. In other words, the venture-income is shared between the owner and shepherd according to some culturally predetermined ratio. In the biblical story of the relations of production between Jacob and his maternal uncle, Laban, this practice was very much in evidence (Genesis 30).

In the traditional Igbo communal setting, it is the general practice and custom for the rich well-to-do farmers who have over-stretched their capability to further expand the sizes of their farms and barns by direct ploughing to obtain or employ the services and cooperation of younger less established farmers. The system is operated in such a way that the rich farmer provides the seedlings, which constitute the venture-capital, while the new hand or less established farmer (the labourer) does the cultivation, tendering, weeding and so on until harvest. The two parties then come together and share the produce of this venture in the normal customarily predetermined ratio, which is usually 2 to 1: capital to labour, and for some items 1 to 1.

In the old Igbo society, this tradition was inculcated in the youth right from their early years. Thus boys of about 5 to 6 years begin that early to be patronized by their older relatives and benefactors alike. A member of the latter category would provide a newly weaned chick (female) to a little lad to tend. When the chick matures into a hen, produces and successfully rears her own chicks until they are weaned, the two parties come together to share these in the normal customarily approved ratio.

A boy who is seen to be good at this semi-pastime or duty stands a good chance of being given higher responsibilities by his sponsor or benefactor. For instance, the relative or benefactor could present him with an ewe'- lamb to rear as he matures. Here, it will be the responsibility of the youth to graze the animal, tethering it in the fields. Again he will be rewarded for this work through the same process of sharing the ewe's off-springs as they get procreated. In this way, young bright boys begin to accumulate capital even from very tender ages.

In the commercial sector, a similar practice obtained and still obtains with respect to the relationship between the established merchants and the younger ones (apprentices) that serve or train under them. To shorten the long story, after about 5-7 years of this master/servant relationship, the merchant cedes some reasonable capital to the apprentice with which he starts his own business.

This practice partially survives to date in the Igbo hinterland and remains a rational progressive format that fuels the people's industry and ability to cope with their environment. The system not only embodies equity but also contains ingredients that dampen recessionary pressure and depression through fair equitable distribution of incomes and wealth. This model of relations of production gave traditional Igbo land a society without unemployment, without prostitutes, without drunkards and without beggars!

Apart from the age-old Igbo village democracy, the above relations of production helped greatly to deepened Igbo egalitarianism. It also made income/wealth distribution in the Igbo homeland to tend towards normal distribution, which by this thesis is a major attribute of the centrist ideology. Is this relations of production not therefore worthy of replication or preservation, say, by adopting it to modernity?

The above socioeconomic model is neither capitalistic nor socialistic; it is centrist. It is structured to make a youngster earn his living primarily through the use of his young muscles and intellect, acquiring capital along the way such that in his middle ages he would progressively earn his living through his labour power, intellect and accumulated capital, and at very old age largely through his accumulated capital. Therefore, what is needed is to give the practice a modern impetus as canvassed in the foregoing, and use same to harness the abundant resources bestowed on the people by nature as well as stabilize the country and advance its development needs and fortune.

In the traditional society as can be gleaned above, relations of production usually involved interplay between a single venture-capitalist and a labourer. But in the more modern systems, we often find a single entrepreneur or venture-capitalist dealing with many labourers or employees sometimes numbering in the thousands. This therefore demands a different set of rules regarding factor-shares as they pertain to Labour and Capital in a modern enterprise, for the simple customarily determined ratios may be out of place here and now.

If we accept the above logic, then we can get on to the next question, which is, HOW and WHO determines the ratio at which LABOUR and CAPITAL should share incomes or the value-added to a business venture?

Economists recognise the existence of two categories of capitalists: the investor, who uses capital to set up productive properties in order to make profit; and the lender who loans out capital in order to earn interest. In the early days, these two categories of capitalists used to fight over interest rates and modes of debt payment. But today, with the intervention of government, such disagreement is hardly noticeable. Modern governments now determine interest rates or provide guidelines for their eventual determination by the banks; and review same from time to time in accordance with certain set down principles. They therefore play the part of umpires by presiding over two competing interests.

By so doing, governments infuse a sense of civility with regard to what may after all be referred to as income distribution between these two "factors" of production. So why can't governments play the same role with respect to income distribution between LABOUR and CAPITAL?

In determining the applicable ratios or percentages that should be used in the modern setting, it is germane that we take cognizance of what applied in the heydays of Western economies after the Great Depression (from about 1938 to about 1980) when there was relative equity and fairness in factor shares. (See, Chart III & Tables 2 & 3). Other factors worthy of consideration in the determination of factor shares as they should apply to Capital and Labour (and indeed a detailed philosophical backgrounding of the centrist ideology) are treated in the book, *Strategy for Political Stability* (2019) pp.109-116 by this author.

Indeed, we go further to say that in stipulating the minimum percentage of company income that should go to the labour force of a company, government should take cognisance of rates that stabilised Western economies and societies in the immediate aftermath of the Great Depression especially when the growth rate of labour shares of national income achieved parity with growth rates in productivity of those economies as shown in Chart I, again between 1938-1980. In Nigeria where employees' compensations have stagnated below 30% in many industries and production outfits, efforts should be made to raise them to about 50%.

Finally, we are reminded that often, real or actual income for a company may not be known until the end of a year. To accommodate this lag in the distribution tangle, we need to introduce a form of living allowance payable to each worker every month pending the time (end of the year or every half-year) when final audited account/income is ready, when the actual labour share of the added-value is known.

In sum, it is our contention that the application of these rules to our socioeconomic management policies will lead to a clustering of the vast majority of the people around the mean or mode of the society's income/wealth frequency distribution curve while a small percentage will be left on its tapering extremities. In other words, there will emerge a strong and vibrant middle class in the society, with fewer people in the rich and poor classes; which is another way of saying that wealth/income distribution will increasingly tend towards the *normal distribution* pattern.

TABLE 2.

Percentage shares of employee compensation in different countries, 1938 – 68

	1938	1948	1958	1968
Belgium	45	52	57	62
Canada	63	63	68	71
France	50	54a	59	63
W. Germany (A)	54	58b	60	64
Ireland	54	51	56	60
Japan	39	42a	52	54
Norway	55	58	65	68
Sweden (B)	52	61	66	72
UK	63	70	73	75
USA	67	64	71	72

Sources: 1938, 1948, 1958 from Heidensohn (1969), Table

1. 1968 from the International Labour Office,
Yearbook of labour statistics, 1971, Table 24
Notes: [a]1949,
        [b]1950

Estimates are for the share of employee compensation in national income except where indicated A (share in net domestic product) and B (share in gross national product).
See also Nwankwo, Uchenna, Economic Agenda for Nigeria (1992) p. 24

TABLE 3.

Percentage shares of national income, United States, 1930-1980

Year	Employee Compensation	Self-Employment income**	Profit and interest**	Rent+	Adjusted share of labour++
	%	%	%	%	%
1930	63	16	15	6	75
1935	66	19	12	3	81
1940	65	16	15	4	77
1945	68	18	12	2	83
1950	66	16	15	3	79
1955	69	13	15	3	79
1960	72	11	14	3	81
1965	70	10	17	3	78
1970	76	8	13	3	83
1975	77	7	14	2	83
1980	75	6	17	2	80

* The figures have been adjusted so that the shares add to 100 per cent.

** With stock appreciation and capital consumption adjustments.

? With capital consumption adjustment.

++ Calculated on basis of 'economy-wide' shares. Sources: Statistical Abstract of the United States 1980, Table 734, and Survey of Current Business, December

1981, Table 10.3. See also Atkinson, A. B, The Economics of Inequality (1983). See also Nwankwo, Uchenna, Economic Agenda for Nigeria (1992) p. 250

PART III
SOCIO-POLITICAL FORMAT

CHAPTER 6

ELEMENTARY & SECONDARY DISTRIBUTION OF POLITICAL POWER

Elementary Distribution of Political Power

Just as the mode of distribution of economic power or wealth may affect the liberty of the individual in a society so also could the mode of distribution of political power. It is a truism that where wealth or power is concentrated in few hands, the stability of the society and the liberties of its individuals could in the final analysis be jeopardised.

Distribution of political power amongst individuals in any given polity herein referred to as elementary or primary distribution of political power is dependent on the form of government in operation. Traditionally, three distinct forms of government have evolved in mankind's long and chequered history of political posturing and inquiry. These are: monarchy, aristocracy and democracy. For purposes of clarity, we need restate the meanings or definitions of these labels, appraise each of them and weigh the relevance or appropriateness of each of them in the light of this thesis.

MONARCHY

Monarchy is probably the earliest form of government known to man. Ancient history is replete with the travails of monarchical rule. Simply put, monarchy is government by one man. Theoretically the monarch is not subject to legal limitations and is therefore free to do things according to his own will. He is the absolute ruler, a potentate. Thus, monarchical rule involves the concentration of political power in one single individual. However, the extent of power a monarch might possess or wield varies from one to the other depending on whether it is an absolute monarchy, constitutional monarchy, etc. It can also be hereditary with father or mother passing the throne onto one of their offspring.

Although monarchy is often differentiated into two forms: absolute and constitutional, our focus here is on the former as the latter, constitutional monarchy, involves a power-sharing arrangement between the monarch and parliament or the representatives of the people. The constitutional monarch has to seek the consent of the representative bodies, accept advice from ministers, respect the letters of the Constitution, etc. In which case, it may well be argued that constitutional monarchy is no monarchy in the real sense of the word.

Indeed, there are many arguments that can be tabled against and for monarchical rule but looked upon from the standpoint of equitable or fair distribution of power, which is of central interest and concern to us here, monarchy can hardly be recommended since it represents the concentration of political power in only one man instead of striving at the attainment of a spread that might approach normal distribution. Also to be brought under this purview is the more modern concept of totalitarianism, in which the ruler is an absolute dictator that is not restricted by a constitution or laws or opposition elements.

ARISTOCRACY

Aristocracy is government by a few individuals that constitute themselves into a ruling class. It is the second form of government evolved by man. The aristocrat is not bound to seek the opinion or support of the ruled for it is presumed that they (the aristocrats) possess superior knowledge and intellect to deal with the affairs of the nation or community without recourse to a people's mandate.

Despite the fact that aristocracy embraces a wider dispersion of power than monarchy, it is still bedevilled by most of the points raised against monarchy. Its chances of success are again dependent on the benevolence of its operators. Where these fellows are not equal to the task, aristocracy becomes (like monarchy) a terrible burden. In this sense, it could degenerate into oligarchy.

Furthermore, aristocracy (like Monarchy) is weakened by problems arising from succession. Because its members virtually have to occupy their positions for life, an element of rigidity and conservatism always bedevil aristocratic governments thereby making them un-adaptive to changing social and economic conditions. Thus, while it is desirable to have the best men always at the decision-taking levels of government, aristocracy cannot be recommended because of these limitations.

Anyway, going by this thesis, the fact that aristocracy involves a very high degree of concentration of power in few hands, it cannot be recommended by the centrist or form part of the centrist ideology.

DEMOCRACY

Democracy is a form of government in which the citizens exercise the governing power either directly or through their elected representatives who may be changed or re-elected periodically. Thus, a state is termed democratic if she has institutions for the expression of the people's supremacy and right to self-determination on vital questions of social direction and policy.[1] It is the third and perhaps the most popular of all the forms of government known to man.

Constitutionally, democracy is expressed by the provision of equal rights for all normal adults to vote and stand for elections; periodic elections; freedom of speech and association, etc. In so far as these rules or rights provide opportunities for mass political participation, it can be said that democracy makes for dispersed power. And that all things being equal it approximates the normal distribution of power which by this thesis is a cardinal requirement for lasting social cohesion and political stability. Democracy cannot therefore be criticised on these grounds.

Theoretically, democracy is superior to the other two forms of government. It gives to every person, a sense of responsibility and recognition, while at the same time ensuring that his interests or rights are not whimsically disregarded. Thus, where anyone is genuinely interested in pursuing his legitimate interests and possesses the ability so to do, he cannot be discounted. It gives all men, theoretically speaking, equal access to power and voice in the affairs of the community.

---

1. A. Appadorai, *The Substance of Politics*, Op. Cit. Page 137

Furthermore, democracy provides possibility for a nonviolent change of government. Where the existing government is found wanting, an election can readily provide an alternative government. Even where a government is not changed, realisation of the ever-present possibility of change, presumably makes those in power to work harder and more conscientiously for group or societal goals. This therefore, checks the tendency to corruption and decadence, making the pursuance of common interest and welfare uppermost in the minds of those in power. In this sense, democracy makes authority a trust.

Because democracy allows for the freedom of opinion and association amongst others, it guarantees the safety of the individual from internal enemies. It curtails effectively the possibility of using state power against anyone. Where these safeguards do not exist as in monarchy and aristocracy, any form of dissent may be misconstrued and punished accordingly. In the light of all these, one can say that even if democracy may not be referred to as the ideal government, it must be recognised as the best alternative. While one may not deny that it could possess characteristics that could be negative to proper social and political organisation, it must be pointed out that when appropriately harnessed, it stands to guarantee a most lasting and healthy polity.

Deficiencies of democracy lie mainly on its applicability and workability in societies where there are high rates of illiteracy, low political consciousness, social and economic inequalities, etc. Where these conditions exist, democracy may appear indeed to be government by ignorant fools as some critics often say. Therefore, to make for true democracy, it is necessary to eliminate or push to the barest minimum the existence in society of the above-mentioned maladies. As for the criticism that the rule of the majority is not necessarily the rule of the best ideas; that the majority is not always right, one can only quip that the rule of the minority as represented by monarchy and aristocracy does not fare any better in this direction. They can be found wanting on that score too since the minority can also be wrong.

Finally, democracy is widely criticised on the grounds that it carries within it a supposedly ill-fated component; the party system. The point put forward against the party system is that it encourages insincerity and intellectual dishonesty because in the bid to abide by party norms and rules, the party-man could become so loyal to the party that the interests of the larger society is compromised or relegated to the background thereby paving the way for undue exploitation of the community by certain individuals within the party.

Although the question of party: to be or not to be, is peripheral to the central issue of what form of government is best suited for a society, it nevertheless cannot be overlooked. However, while one may agree to some extent with the point against the party system, it has to be pointed out that the system has its strong points. In the first place, to the extent that the party is organised principally upon the basic criterion that the interests, aims and opinions of its members are identical and therefore worthy of pursuit in a collective way, the party spirit appears natural to the democratic process. It marks the accentuation of the old adage that birds of the same feather flock together. In other words, a form of ganging up is inevitable in democratic politics if not in all societal processes.

Furthermore, it must be recognised that the party system fulfils certain basic functions that are necessary for the sustenance of democratic politics. This is the vital need for organisation and for the identification and articulation of the muted interests and opinions of the people, as a guide to the formulation and presentation of principles and policies upon which a popular and viable government may be constructed. It also represents a forum for educating the electorate politically in order to reduce the chances of having governments elected and perhaps run by fools.

The party also helps to maintain a sense of continuity in public policy. Where the party does not exist, it is conceivable that each successive government being moulded upon an individual would entail widely varying policies. The party system also works against ethnic or tribal politics especially where there are two or more parties and the constitution demands fair national spread from the parties. Also, the two-party or multi-party system helps to keep the government of the day in check, for in the absence of an organised opposition as represented by the other party, it would be very difficult to change or bring pressure upon the incumbent administration in any decisive way. Thus, a dictatorship might result.

Arguably, two brands of Democracy thrive side by side in the now world: the two or multi-party democracy and the one-party democracy, with their respective merits and demerits. But what is recognised here or by the centrist as democratic is the two-party or multi-party system.

SECONDARY DISTRIBUTION OF POLITICAL POWER

Just as a fair distribution of political power among individuals in a polity may favourably affect the degree of freedom the citizens enjoy and the likely degree of cohesion, understanding, solidarity and oneness of a people, so could the perceived fairness in the distribution of power amongst the ethnic groups or sub-national entities – states, regions, etc. – that make up that polity do the same. Where political power is perceived to rest mainly with one section of the populace, the other section or sections are likely to show resentment about the status quo. In extreme cases, this could lead to protestations against the status quo, agitations for change, separatist movements and even civil wars.

As a result of this, the mode of power distribution among ethnic or sub-national groups in a country has always been of central concern and importance to nation-builders and ideologues. It is widely recognised that a good or fair power-sharing arrangement is crucial in the process of organising and building a nation. Hence, over the years, there have emerged different power sharing models in the governance of countries or nations. Before we can make any meaningful statement as to the appropriateness of this or that system or mode of power distribution among sub-national or ethnic groups in national politics, we need first to examine the existing models, their evolution, acceptability and relevance to prevailing realities.

MODES OF POWER DISTRIBUTION AMONGST (ETHNIC) GROUPS IN NATIONAL POLITICS

Ever since the dawn of democratic government in the Greek City-States and its subsequent adaptation by emergent country-states, there has been steady development in the modes of power-sharing and distribution arrangements between communal or territorial groups that have come to make up modem nation-states. In the Greek city-states, the problems of ethnicity – its demand for power-sharing and communal political participation – were largely absent because the polis, as the Greeks called their states were comparatively small, both in land area and population. And because the inhabitants of each state were practically of the same stock, each city-state boiled down to what we may today refer to as a single constituency.

On the other hand, the largeness of the modern country-state with its often heterogeneous groups, differentiated from one another in intricate and diverse ways, coupled with the attendant divergence in interests, opinions, goals, etc. makes political organisation and the process of mustering consensus and solidarity, a complex and sometimes wary business. As such, nation-builders have come to realise that the smaller geographic territories, ethnic or communal groups and the political power elites who govern them cannot be ignored if a truly strong and virile nation-state is to emerge or is to be sustained from the aggregation of communities or ethnic groups who usually make up the modern country-state.

In turn, this has led to the obvious conclusion, that some sort of acceptable power-sharing and distribution scheme is necessary in the large country-states not only for the sake of preserving and accommodating certain differences in the cultures of the different units but also to ensure reasonable and commensurate communal political participation at the centre. This is viewed now as the only lasting and peaceful method to achieving and maintaining a true nation-state where a high degree of passionate identification and allegiance to the centre is necessary to overcome the numerous internal differences of the units that often jeopardise national stability and survival. Needless to say, it is a truism that without creating the proper national political climate upon which the appropriate national sentiment can be built, the equation of a country-state to a nation-state would forever remain suspect, as the former is more of a geographical expression while the latter is basically a political concept.

In keeping with the above, two basic patterns of organising and institutionalising national power have thus far emerged. The first is the establishment of tiers of government and the second is the concept of assuring, even if to different degrees, that adequate political participation at the centre is not denied any community. The creation of tiers of government is borne out of the tendency or desire to preserve and accommodate regional cultural differences. It is therefore designed to deal with what areas of policy-making or governance the different tiers of government or groups are to preside. The direct result of this concern is the emergence and survival of the Unitary and Federal systems of government.

Generally, it must be observed, where the units are powerful and the people tend to cling to their different communal traditions, the federal system is more favourable, while the unitary system is usually adopted in places where the units are either weak or possess relatively homogeneous cultural traditions. The United States, India and Nigeria are typical examples of countries that chose to be organised on the principles of the federal system from inception or independence, while Guyana, Haiti, Panama, etc., represent typical unitary states.

The above precepts of unitary/federal systems and the concepts of unicameral and bicameral legislatures or of single-chamber/ two-chamber parliaments which usually accompany them respectively have no doubt led to equitable distribution of power that have helped stabilise many a polity. We endorse these arrangements wholesale.

As an aside, let me state that although Nigeria opted for federalism at independence in 1960, it has now been turned into a unitary state that is merely masquerading as a federation. This is the handiwork of a minority group intent on foisting itself as the master race in the country by subjecting the rest of the country under its whim. This new status of the country comes with tremendous friction, and the heat so generated by the friction is daily rising in scope and at such a pace that if care is not taken it would turn into a major conflagration in the foreseeable future, with dire consequences for the country.

The point is that running complex and heterogeneous Nigeria as a unitary state instead of a federation, which augurs well with its large size and diversity, is causing a lot of hiccups in that country. It is easy to see that unless Nigeria is returned to functional federalism, the present political turbulence in the country will persist, in fact deepen.

CHAPTER 7

TERTIARY DISTRIBUTION OF POLITICAL POWER

From the foregoing, it is clear that although the issue of distribution of political power among subnational groups in a polity has long been settled – at least at the theoretical level – at the third and last frontier, the world stage, the issue of equitable distribution of power amongst nations or countries of the world has remained rather uncharted. Indeed, as Roger D. Masters once observed, world politics remains a primitive political system (See, Masters, Roger D, *World Politics as a Primitive Political System*, published by Princeton University Press, 1964). And as nation-states are being pulled together into a global community by massive developments in Science and Technology, the telling effect of this primitive politics and its accompanying lack of order is increasing in leaps and bounds.

That the United Nations (UN) is largely ineffective in tackling problems of insecurity and peaceful coexistence on the globe; problems of environmental pollution and other problems of common nature to mankind is partly due to this unsettled issue because it helps boost anarchic tendencies on the planet. The present system that leaves such matters to a few selected countries in the Security Council – to the virtual exclusion of the United Nations General Assembly (UNGA) – leaves much to be desired, more so since the composition of that council and the frequent use of the veto to block decisions in the Security Council constitutes a stumbling block to progress of any sort.

Of course, one problem that makes the UNGA irrelevant in the present scheme of things is that there exists within the Assembly a kind of utopian equality of member-states such that powerful nations like the United States, which produces nearly a quarter of world goods and services and China with a population of nearly one-fifth of the world total are given equal votes with little powerless nations in the Assembly. We are of the firm conviction that if an equitable format for power distribution at the international arena is achieved, leading to a proper gradation of voting powers within the UNGA, the Assembly can then function as a World Assembly, and hence be in a better position to make laws that govern the conduct of nations instead of leaving such matters to the intrigues-ridden UN Security Council, or worse, individual powerful countries that represent themselves instead of any other nations.

In view of the above, the following questions may be asked: what yardsticks should we use for assessing national strength and therefore for expressing the vexed but valid principle that responsibility must be linked to power in international affairs? In other words, how do we propose to distribute or assign statuses and powers to different nations at the UN or a new World Legislature? Would this formula be able to direct men's energies away from the armed race? And finally, would the formula elicit the support of the big-five and so become admissible in the comity of nations?

To answer the first question, we need to delve a little into what we may refer to as the true axiology of national power. Basically, national power or strength is a three-dimensional concept, resting upon:

(I) Economic Power;

(2) Numerical Strength or Population; and

(3) National Will (Capacity for Innovation/Tenacity of purpose)

At the national level, power-sharing between subnational groups – states, regions, etc. – is based roughly on the application of two factors, namely:

(1) the numerical size of each state; and,

(2) the equality of states principle.

But at the international level, we have to add Economic Power to the above two to make up a three-dimensional power-sharing model that should befit the international arena, hence:

(1) Economic Power;

(2) Numerical Strength or Population; and

(3) Equality of States

The relevance of population and economic power needs no elaboration. Willpower, however, refers to that intrinsic quality of being, luck or resilience which could give a group some advantages over the other especially when other factors are held constant. In fact, it corresponds to that same factor upon which the 'equality of states' principle got introduced into power-sharing schemes in national politics. That is, it is same as that factor responsible for the second (upper) chamber or Senate in the national legislature.

Each of these factors contributes to national power and is very vital to national survival at any point in time. When a country possesses a healthy dose of all these three attributes, she becomes really great or dominant and may then channel the enormous powers that derive from these sources into either peaceful or aggressive purposes. If the nation chooses the first option, that is, channelling her immense resources to peaceful pursuits, she would, as things are, turn out to be a benign, affable giant often contributing positively to the welfare of lesser powers and to the progress of mankind, in general. If on the other hand a nation chooses the second option, it could develop an immense and fearsome military machine, intimidating the lesser powers and possibly winning herself a veto-status by the existing scheme of things.

By way of definition, a nation's economic power relative to another may be estimated from the size of their respective G.N.P or G.D.P. The economic power of a nation affects the ultimate strength of that country in diverse ways. For one thing, it partly determines the value, quality or quantity of goods (military or non-military) and services a country can produce or acquire, the degree to which that society can sustain the welfare or material needs of her populace and to some extent the state of evolution of her material culture.

The numerical strength or population of a country on the other hand, reflects the number of individuals in that country and the probable 'manpower' she can deploy in the pursuit of any task or goal, be it peaceful or aggressive. Hence, in a war as well as in peace time, the available number of men needed to operate the nation's available weapons or machines of industry, and to take any actions, tangible or intangible, necessary for the pursuit of the nation's goals, depends on that country's population. It is therefore no surprise that where all other factors are constant, population becomes the crucial determinant of which nation is mightier.

Finally, national will, which informs the concept of equality of states, deals with a people's resolve and determination to pursue any chosen line of action and make the best of it. It roughly equates to Capacity for Innovation/ Tenacity of purpose. National-will may be embedded in belief systems, moral, philosophical and theological inclinations of a people. It may also be anchored on a feeling of self-righteousness or upon the experiences of a people. Whatever the foundations upon which a people's will may hinge, Will-power, unlike the other two factors is basically a subjective concept which is not amenable to empirical measurement. Any attempt to give national Will-power an objective analysis is illusory and may land us onto the threshold of ethnocentrism. However, that does not obviate the fact that different peoples at different times possess different degrees of Will-power or tenacity of purpose which energises and galvanises their beings into great and extra-ordinary actions and achievements.

The intrinsic relationship and inter-dependence of these three factors is not debatable. That they feed into one another in diverse and intricate ways is sure. While each is extremely significant, taken together they prove irresistibly presage. They form the tripod upon which a nation's true power rests. And it is from this power that military might could flow. Where any of the three factors is weak we find that the potency of the country's power, military and otherwise, is suspect.

Military might apart, the USA and Russia can lay claim to super-power status because they each have a strong economic base buttressed by advanced technological know-how, and at least the optimal population to back up such development. China, with its present number two status as an economic power and an overwhelming population figure cannot be ignored in this regard.

On the other hand, and despite their respective strong economic and technological base, Britain and France suffer from relative low population count, though they are influential enough to mobilise manpower support and assistance from around the world. Saudi Arabia with all her petro-dollars lacks the right size of population that is a sine qua non to global greatness. Despite its ranking fourth position on the world population index, Indonesia's greatness and global reach is fractured by her relatively weak economic and technological base.

On the basis of the above, we feel strongly that national economic power, population and will-power represent the real factors upon which national power rests. To deviate from these axioms and equate national power or responsibility to national military capability is in our considered opinion fraudulent, short-sighted and dangerous. It is fraudulent because industrial and economic giants like Japan and Germany which could literally build themselves monstrous military machines overnight are denied their rightful place in the scheme of things and the comity of nations.

It is short-sighted because the probable consequences of that mode of assigning 'responsibility' are not taken into consideration. And finally, it is dangerous because it taunts such truly great nations like Japan, Germany, India, Brazil, etc., and could subsequently draw them into the arms race, big time. What is more, if a country is capable of contributing to a relatively large portion of the world's economic well-being and material progress, then it stands to reason that she should be given some prominence in the world community.

Surely, we should not wait until countries like Japan begin to build themselves monstrous military capability before we start to assign them positions commensurate with their true powers in the comity of nations.

POWER SHARING WITHIN THE PROPOSED WORLD ASSEMBLY OR THE NEW UNITED NATIONS

We have established that the voting power of each nation should be based on the nation's economic power, population and will-power. These form the true determinants of a nation's real strength – and ultimately underlines the degree to which her military strength can be raised. Pursuant to this therefore, we suggest that in the proposed world legislature, these three factors should be used to weight each country's vote.

To achieve this, it would be necessary to express the economic power and population of every country as a percentage of the world's total. The economic power of a country can of course be based on her Gross National Product and Gross Domestic Product, etc., or a combination of these. Having done this, we can regard the percentage point derived from any of the three factors as representing the power contributed to that nation's ultimate voting power by the particular factor. We then proceed to sum up these three figures and find the average score by dividing the sum by three. The ensuing figure should then be taken as the country's voting power within the legislature.

Thus, if we propose a World Legislature of about 1,000 members then we simply multiply the country's voting power by 1,000 and divide by 100 to get the number of seats the country would have in the World Legislature or Assembly.

Note that because the third factor is subjective, we cannot afford to be discriminatory in its distribution. Each nation therefore is on this count assigned equal weight. Thus, using the 233 countries in the latest UN ranking of World population, then each country is assigned 100/233 percentage point or 0.43% as the share of each country on the Equality of States (National Will) factor.

By way of illustration, we shall proceed to compute the Voting Power of all countries in the world or demonstrate what the distribution of voting strength that would result from the application of the suggested principle. But first, we shall calculate that of China and the USA as a guide:

1. **China**

    Statistics show that this country produced about US$13,407.398 trillion worth of goods and services per year or 16.25% of the entire world's GDP in 2018, which therefore represents her score on the Economic Power scale for the given year. World GDP for 2018 is put at US$84,740.322 trillion – IMF.

The Chinese population is known to be about 1,420,062,022 which is about 18.41 % (2019), of the world total representing the score of China on the Population Index. The World Population is put at about 7,577,130,400 at the point of this measurement. (Source: Worldometers (www.Worldometers.info) Elaboration of data by United Nations, Department of Economic and Social Affairs, Population Division.).

Finally, the country scores another 0.43% (i.e. 100÷233) % from the third factor, i.e. national-will or Equality of States Index (EQI).

Therefore, the Voting Power (V.P) for China in the propose World Legislature comes to this;

$$V.P = \frac{16.25 + 18.41 + 0.43}{3} = 11.7\%$$

By multiplying 11.7 by 10 (or 1,000÷100) we arrive at 117, which represents the number of Seats assignable to China in the proposed World Parliament for the year 2019.

2. United States of America

Statistics show that this country produced about US$20,494.050 trillion worth of goods and services per year or 24.19% of the entire world's GDP in 2018, which therefore represents her score on the Economic Power scale for the given year, World GDP for 2018 being put at US$84,740.322 trillion.

The US population is known to be about 329,093,110 (2019), which is about 4.27% of the world total representing the score of USA on the Population Index. The World Population is put at about 7,577,130,400. (Source: Worldometers (www.Worldometers.info) Elaboration of data by United Nations, Department of Economic and Social Affairs, Population Division.).
Finally, the country scores another 0.43% (i.e., 100 ÷233) % from the third factor, i.e. national-will or Equality of States Index (EQI).

Therefore, the Voting Power (V.P) for the USA in the propose World Legislature comes to this;

$$V.P = \frac{24.19 + 4.27 + 0.43}{3} = 9.63\%$$

By multiplying 9.63 by 10 (1000÷100) we arrive at 96, which represents the number of Seats assignable to the USA in the proposed World Parliament for the year 2019.

VOTING POWER/SEATS FOR COUNTRIES IN THE PROPOSED WORLD LEGISLATURE

We now publish hereunder the projected voting powers/ seats for all the countries of the world in the proposed World Legislature as calculated from the formula suggested in this book:

TABLE 6.1
Distribution of Seats for Countries in the Proposed World Assembly, Legislature or Parliament

Using the above formula, the Voting Power / Seats for Countries of the World in the Proposed World Legislature or Parliament can be shown to be as follows:

No	Country	% of World Pop	% of World GDP	EQI %	Total Score (TS)%	Voting Power (TS÷3)	Seats
1	China	18.41	16.25	0.43	35.09	11.7	117
2.	USA	4.27	24.19	"	28.89	9.63	96
3.	India	17.74	3.21	"	21.38	7.13	71
4.	Japan	1.64	5.87	"	8.02	2.67	27
5.	Germany	1.07	4.72	"	6.22	2.07	21
6.	Brazil	2.75	2.21	"	5.39	1.80	18
7.	Indonesia	3.49	1.21	"	5.13	1.71	17
8.	UK	0.87	3.34	"	4.64	1.55	16
9	France	0.85	3.28	"	4.56	1.52	15
10.	Russia	1.87	1.92	"	4.22	1.41	14
11.	Italy	0.77	2.45	"	3.65	1.22	12
12.	Mexico	1.72	1.44	"	3.59	1.20	12
13.	Nigeria	2.60	0.47	"	3.50	1.17	12
14.	Pakistan	2.65	0.37	"	3.45	1.15	12

15.	South Korea	0.67	1.91	"	3.01	1.00	10
16.	Bangladesh	2.18	0.34	"	2.95	0.98	10
17.	Canada	0.48	2.02	"	2.93	0.98	10
18.	Spain	0.60	1.68	"	2.71	0.90	9
19.	Australia	0.33	1.67	"	2.43	0.81	8
20.	Turkey	1.08	0.90	"	2.41	0.80	8
21.	Philippines	1.40	0.39	"	2.22	0.74	7
22	Iran	1.07	0.53	"	2.03	0.68	7
23.	Egypt	1.31	0.29	"	2.03	0.68	7
24.	Vietnam	1.26	0.29	"	1.98	0.66	7
25.	Ethiopia	1.43	0.10	"	1.96	0.65	7
26.	Thailand	0.90	0.58	"	1.91	0.64	6
27.	Saudi Arabia	0.44	0.92	"	1.79	0.60	6
28.	Netherlands	0.22	1.08	"	1.73	0.60	6
29.	Argentina	0.58	0.61	"	1.62	0.54	5
30.	Poland	0.49	0.69	"	1.61	0.54	5
31.	South Africa	0.75	0.43	"	1.61	0.54	5
32.	DR. Congo	1.12	0.05	"	1.60	0.53	5
33.	Colombia	0.65	0.39	"	1.47	0.49	5
34.	Taiwan	0.31	0.70	"	1.44	0.48	5
35.	Switzerland	0.11	0.83	"	1.37	0.46	5
36	Tanzania	0.79	0.07	"	1.29	0.43	4
37.	Malaysia	0.42	0.42	"	1.27	0.42	4
38.	Iraq	0.52	0.26	"	1.22	0.41	4
39.	Kenya	0.68	0.11	"	1.22	0.41	4

40.	Sweden	0.13	0.65	"	1.21	0.40	4
41.	Belgium	0.15	0.63	"	1.21	0.40	4
42.	Myanmar	0.70	0.08	"	1.21	0.40	4
43.	Algeria	0.55	0.21	"	1.19	0.40	4
44.	Ukraine	0.57	0.14	"	1.14	0.38	4
45.	Peru	0.43	0.27	"	1.13	0.38	4
46.	Austria	0.11	0.54	"	1.08	0.36	4
47.	UAE	0.13	0.50	"	1.06	0.35	4
48.	Uganda	0.59	0.03	"	1.05	0.35	4
49.	Morocco	0.47	0.14	"	1.04	0.35	4
50.	Chile	0.24	0.35	"	1.02	0.34	3
51.	Sudan	0.55	0.04	"	1.02	0.34	3
52.	Norway	0.07	0.51	"	1.02	0.34	3
53.	Israel	0.11	0.43	"	0.97	0.32	3
54.	Angola	0.41	0.13	"	0.97	0.32	3
55.	Venezuela	0.42	0.12	"	0.97	0.32	3
56.	Hong Kong	0.10	0.43	"	0.96	0.32	3
57.	Romania	0.25	028	"	0.96	0.32	3
58.	Singapore	0.08	0.43	"	0.94	0.31	3
59.	Ireland	0.06	0.44	"	0.93	0.31	3
60.	Afghanistan	0.48	0.02	"	0.93	0.31	3
61.	Denmark	0.07	0.41	"	0.91	0.30	3
62.	Uzbekistan	0.43	0.05	"	0.91	0.30	3
63.	Ghana	0.39	0.08	"	0.90	0.30	3

64.	Kazakhstan	0.20	0.24	"	0.87	0.29	3
65	Czech Republic	0.14	0.29	"	0.86	0.29	3
66.	Mozambique	0.41	0.02	"	0.86	0.29	3
67.	Nepal	0.39	0.03	"	0.85	0.28	3
68.	Portugal	0.13	0.28	"	0.84	0.28	3
69.	Yemen	0.38	0.03	"	0.84	0.28	3
70.	Finland	0.07	0.33	"	0.83	0.28	3
71.	Greece	0.14	0.26	"	0.83	0.28	3
72.	Cote d'Ivore	0.33	0.05	"	0.81	0.27	3
73.	Cameroon	033	0.05	"	0.81	0.27	3
74.	Sri Lanka	0.27	0.01	"	0.80	0.26	3
75.	Madagascar	0.35	0.01	"	0.79	0.26	3
76.	Ecuador	0.22	0.13	"	0.78	0.25	3
77.	Syria	0.24	0.09	"	0.76	0.25	3
78.	Guatemala	0.23	0.09	"	0.75	0.25	3
79.	Hungary	0.13	0.18	"	0.74	0.25	3
80.	Niger	0.30	0.01	"	0.74	0.25	3
81.	New Zeeland	0.06	0.24	"	0.73	0.24	2
82.	Mali	0.26	0.02	"	0.71	0.24	2
83.	Burkina Faso	0.26	0.02	"	0.71	0.24	2
84.	Qatar	0.04	0.23	"	0.70	0.23	2
85.	Zambia	0.24	0.03	"	0.70	0.23	2
86.	Malawi	0.26	0.00	"	0.69	0.23	2
87.	Zimbabwe	0.22	0.03	"	0.68	0.23	2
88.	Senegal	0.22	0.03	"	0.68	0.23	2
89.	Dominican Rep.	0.14	0.10	"	0.67	0.22	2
90.	Cambodia	0.21	0.03	"	0.67	0.22	2

91.	Kuwait	0.06	0.17	"	0.66	0.22	2
92.	Chad	0.20	0.01	"	0.64	0.21	2
93.	Slovakia	0.07	0.13	"	0.63	0.21	2
94.	Bolivia	0.15	0.05	"	0.63	0.21	2
95.	Tunisia	0.15	0.05	"	0.63	0.21	2
96.	Belarus	0.12	0.07	"	0.62	0.21	2
97.	Azerbaijan	0.13	0.05	"	0.61	0.20	2
98.	Jordan	0.13	0.01	"	0.61	0.20	2
99.	Guinea	0.17	0.01	"	0.61	0.20	2
100.	Rwanda	0.17	0.01	"	0.61	0.20	2
101.	Puerto Rico	0.05	0.12	"	0.60	0.20	2
102.	Serbia	0.11	0.06	"	0.60	0.20	2
103.	Bulgaria	0.09	0.08	"	0.60	0.20	2
104.	South Sudan	0.17	0.00	"	0.60	0.20	2
105.	Oman	0.06	0.10	"	0.59	0.20	2
106.	Benin	0.15	0.01	"	0.59	0.20	2
107.	Haiti	0.15	0.01	"	0.59	0.20	2
108.	Lebanon	0.08	0.07	"	0.58	0.19	2
109.	Honduras	0.12	0.03	"	0.58	0.19	2
110.	Burundi	0.15	0.00	"	0.58	0.19	2
111.	Libya	0.09	0.05	"	0.57	0.19	2
112.	Paraguay	0.09	0.05	"	0.57	0.19	2
113.	Papua New Guinea	0.11	0.03	"	0.57	0.19	2
114.	Panama	0.05	0.08	"	0.56	0.19	2
115.	Costa Rica	0.06	0.07	"	0.56	0.19	2
116.	Turkmenistan	0.08	0.05	"	0.56	0.19	2
117.	Croatia	0.05	0.07	"	0.55	0.18	2

118.	Uruguay	0.05	0.07	"	0.55	0.18	2
119.	Tajikistan	0.12	0.00	"	0.55	0.18	2
120.	El Salvador	0.08	0.03	"	0.54	0.18	2
121.	Laos	0.09	0.02	"	0.54	0.18	2
122.	Togo	0.11	0.00	"	0.54	0.18	2
123.	Lithuania	0.04	0.06	"	0.54	0.18	2
124.	Nicaragua	0.08	0.02	"	0.53	0.18	2
125.	Sierra Leone	0.10	0.00	"	0.53	0.18	2
126.	Luxemburg	0.01	0.08	"	0.53	0.17	2
127.	Slovenia	0.03	0.06	"	0.52	0.17	2
128.	Congo- The Rep of	0.07	0.01	"	0.52	0.17	2
129.	Kyrgyzstan	0.08	0.00	"	0.51	0.17	2
130.	Macau	0.01	0.06	"	0.50	0.17	2
131.	Bahrain	0.02	0.05	"	0.50	0.17	2
132.	Bosnia & Herzegovina	0.05	0.02	"	0.50	0.17	2
133.	Georgia	0.05	0.02	"	0.50	0.17	2
134.	Eritrea	0.07	0.00	"	0.50	0.17	2
135.	Latvia	0.02	0.04	"	0.49	0.16	2
136.	Estonia	0.02	0.04	"	0.49	0.16	2
137.	Jamaica	0.04	0.02	"	0.49	0.16	2
138.	Albania	0.04	0.02	"	0.49	0.16	2
139.	Mongolia	0.04	0.02	"	0.49	0.16	2

140.	Armenia	0.04	0.02	"	0.49	0.16	2
141.	Moldova	0.05	0.01	"	0.49	0.16	2
142.	Mauritania	0.06	0.00	"	0.49	0.16	2
143.	Liberia	0.06	0.00	"	0.49	0.16	2
144.	Central African Republic	0.06	0.00	"	0.49	0.16	2
145.	Cyprus	0.02	0.03	"	0.48	0.16	2
146.	Trinidad & Tobago	0.02	0.03	"	0.48	0.16	2
147.	Botswana	0.03	0.02	"	0.48	0.16	2
148.	Gabon	0.03	0.02	"	0.48	0.16	2
149.	Namibia	0.03	0.02	"	0.48	0.16	2
150.	Equatorial Guinea	0.03	0.02	"	0.48	0.16	2
151.	North Macedonia	0.03	0.02	"	0.48	0.16	2
152.	Mauritius	0.02	0.02	"	0.47	0.16	2
153.	Iceland	0.00	0.03	"	0.46	0.15	2
154.	Malta	0.01	0.02	"	0.46	0.15	2
155.	Brunei	0.01	0.02	"	0.46	0.15	2
156.	Bahamas, The	0.01	0.02	"	0.46	0.15	2
157.	Lesotho	0.03	0.00	"	0.46	0.15	2
158.	Gambia, The	0.03	0.00	"	0.46	0.15	2
159.	Guinea-Bissau	0.03	0.00	"	0.46	0.15	2
160.	Timor-Leste	0.02	0.00	"	0.45	0.15	2
161.	Montenegro	0.01	0.00	"	0.44	0.15	2
162.	Maldives	0.01	0.00	"	0.44	0.15	2

163.	Fiji	0.01	0.00	"	0.44	0.15	2
164.	Guyana	0.01	0.00	"	0.44	0.15	2
165.	Suriname	0.01	0.00	"	0.44	0.15	2
166.	Bhutan	0.01	0.00	"	0.44	0.15	2
167.	Djibouti	0.01	0.00	"	0.44	0.15	2
168.	Cape Verde	0.01	0.00	"	0.44	0.15	2
169.	Belize	0.01	0.00	"	0.44	0.15	2
170.	Solomon Islands	0.01	0.00	"	0.44	0.15	2
171.	Comoros	0.01	0.00	"	0.44	0.15	2
172.	Micronesia, Fed. State of	0.01	0.00	"	0.44	0.15	2
173.	Barbados	0.00	0.00	"	0.43	0.14	1
174.	St. Lucia	0.00	0.00	"	0.43	0.14	1
175.	San Marino	0.00	0.00	"	0.43	0.14	1
176.	Antigua & Barbud	0.00	0.00	"	0.43	0.14	1
177.	Seychelles	0.00	0.00	"	0.43	0.14	1
178.	Granada	0.00	0.00	"	0.43	0.14	1
179.	St. Kitts & Nevis	0.00	0.00	"	0.43	0.14	1
180.	Vanuatu	0.00	0.00	"	0.43	0.14	1
181.	Samoa	0.00	0.00	"	0.43	0.14	1
182.	St. Vincent & Grenadines	0.00	0.00	"	0.43	0.14	1
183.	Dominica	0.00	0.00	"	0.43	0.14	1

184.	Tonga	0.00	0.00	"	0.43	0.14	1
185.	Sao Tome and Principe	0.00	0.00	"	0.43	0.14	1
186.	Palau	0.00	0.00	"	0.43	0.14	1
187.	Marshall Islands	0.00	0.00	"	0.43	0.14	1
188.	Kiribati	0.00	0.00	"	0.43	0.14	1
189.	Tuvalu	0.00	0.00	"	0.43	0.14	1
	Sub-Total						**953**
	Column B						
190.	Guadeloupe	0.01	N/A	"	0.43	0.14	1
191.	Martinique	0.00	N/A	"	0.43	0.14	1
192.	French Guiana	0.00	N/A	"	0.43	0.14	1
193.	French Polynesia	0.00	N/A	"	0.43	0.14	1
194.	New Caledonia	0.00	N/A	"	0.43	0.14	1
195.	Mayotte	0.00	N/A	"	0.43	0.14	1
196.	Guam	0.00	N/A	"	0.43	0.14	1
197.	Channel Islands	0.00	N/A	"	0.43	0.14	1
198.	Curacao	0.00	N/A	"	0.43	0.14	1
199.	Aruba	0.00	N/A	"	0.43	0.14	1
200.	U.S. Virgin Islands	0.00	N/A	"	0.43	0.14	1

201.	Isle of Man	0.00	N/A	"	0.43	0.14	1
202.	Andorra	0.00	N/A	"	0.43	0.14	1
203.	Cayman Islands	0.00	N/A	"	0.43	0.14	1
204.	Bermuda	0.00	N/A	"	0.43	0.14	1
205.	Greenland	0.00	N/A	"	0.43	0.14	1
206.	American Samoa	0.00	N/A	"	0.43	0.14	1
207.	Northern Mariana Islands	0.00	N/A	"	0.43	0.14	1
208.	Faeroe Islands	0.00	N/A	"	0.43	0.14	1
209.	Saint Maarten	0.00	N/A	"	0.43	0.14	1
210.	Monaco	0.00	N/A	"	0.43	0.14	1
211.	Liechtenstein	0.00	N/A	"	0.43	0.14	1
212.	Turks and Caicos	0.00	N/A	"	0.43	0.14	1
213.	Gibraltar	0.00	N/A	"	0.43	0.14	1
214.	British Virgin Islands	0.00	N/A	"	0.43	0.14	1
215.	Caribbean	0.00	N/A	"	0.43	0.14	1
216.	Cook Islands	0.00	N/A	"	0.43	0.14	1
217.	Anguilla	0.00	N/A	"	0.43	0.14	1
218.	Wallis & Futuna	0.00	N/A	"	0.43	0.14	1
219.	Nauru	0.00	N/A	"	0.43	0.14	1
220.	St. Pierre & Miquelon	0.00	N/A	"	0.43	0.14	1
221.	Montserrat	0.00	N/A	"	0.43	0.14	1

222.	Saint Helena	0.00	N/A	"	0.43	0.14	1
223.	Falkland Islands	0.00	N/A	"	0.43	0.14	1
224.	Niue	0.00	N/A	"	0.43	0.14	1
225.	Tokelau	0.00	N/A	"	0.43	0.14	1
226.	Holy See	0.00	N/A	"	0.43	0.14	1
							953 + 37
	TOTAL						**= 990**
	Column C						
227.	North Korea	0.33	N/A	"	N/A	N/A	N/A
228.	Somalia	0.20	N/A	"	N/A	N/A	N/A
229.	Cuba	0.15	N/A	"	N/A	N/A	N/A
230.	State of Palestine	0.07	N/A	"	N/A	N/A	N/A
231.	Swaziland	0.02	N/A	"	N/A	N/A	N/A
232	Reunion	0.01	N/A	"	N/A	N/A	N/A
233.	Western Sahara	0.01	N/A	"	N/A	N/A	N/A
	GRAND TOTAL						**± 1,000**

Source: GDP is as per data from International Monetary Fund (2018) while the Population data is from Worldometers (www.Worldometers.info) 2019. Elaboration of data by United Nations, Department of Economic and Social Affairs, Population Division.

NB:

The 37 countries in Column B above appeared in this 2019 UN (Worldometer) Population Survey but all scored zeroes as their respective percentage of world population. In the IMF/UN World GDP Survey, they were not featured. If we take that as an indication of dismal economic base, then we can say that they also scored zeroes in this regard. In that respect, they will each qualify – via the Equality Index – to respectively have one seat in the World Parliament as we have so indicated.

That will bring the total number of allotted seats in the Parliament to 953+37 = 990.

Finally, the last 7 countries in Column C are each listed in only one of the two surveys, with marks as shown. Since we do not know their standings on one of the yardsticks for measurement, their actual voting powers are somewhat indeterminate. Suffice it to say that even with the absence of the said missing gradation(s), some of them by virtue of the only one yardstick by which they are ranked are capable of getting 2 or 3 seats in the World Assembly. We expect them in the final analysis to take up the remaining 10 Seats or so to bring the total to about 1,000 Seats.

Please note that no matter how low any country's score or voting power is in the above chart, by virtue of the elasticity of the suggested formula, it is not bound to remain at that level for all time. The figures are not rigid. They are to change according to the yearly performance of each country on the economic and demographic fronts in the future. It is hoped that with the possible and expected change of gear and re-direction of many national development strategy (say from military to non-military pursuits) a fantastic redistribution of voting strength is bound to ensue within a short period of time.

Notice that the USA produced 40 per cent of all industrial goods (and services) in the world in the year 1929, and 25 per cent in 1982 as recorded in the maiden edition of this book that was published in 1988. But now the figure has depreciated to 24.19 per cent. Similarly, the Chinese population accounted for 22.26 per cent of the world total as at 1982 and as recorded in the first edition of this book. But now is 18.41 per cent of the world total. This is just to give a few examples! So, the wheel of life continues to revolve. Today it is here, tomorrow it is there. At one time, Rome was the 'progressive' centre of world, then it shifted to England, and now to the United States. It could be any other state in a couple of decades.

Such is the way of the world, and only those who persevere are likely to hit the top marks and become the respected giants of tomorrow. So, why should one (any nation) despair or kick against this formula simply because it has apparently lowered the erstwhile position of that country on the world's status-scale? It would be a noble act for each and every country, no matter how adversely affected by this proposition, to join hands with other countries to see to the realisation of the suggested scheme.

It is our opinion that once the new voting model takes root, countries will be inclined to spend less on the armament industry, especially once the World Peace Authority begins to reassure us by making noticeable progress in the requisite direction. This will of course begin to alter positions of nations in the above scale and indeed the tendency to maintain large armies and develop new weapon systems would be discouraged.

Finally, we do hereby propose that countries be allowed to produce those that will represent them in the proposed World Assembly or Parliament according to their own traditions. In other words, that democratic countries shall be expected to raise their representatives through elections while governments in non-democratic countries could feel free to handpick or select their own representatives.

ALTERNATIVE B

The way we apply these factors of Population, Equality and Economic Power will depend on what type of Legislature we opt for: whether we take the three factors as equal in every material particular or whether we make some distinctions between them. If we look at these factors as equal and allot equal powers to each, we can easily and conveniently arrive at a Unicameral Legislature. On the other hand, if we make any distinctions between them, then a Tri-cameral Legislature would suggest itself.

GRADATION OF THE THREE FACTORS/INDICES OF LEGISLATIVE REPRESENTATION & TRI-CAMERAL LEGISLATURE

But let us face it, in the bicameral legislature of National Assemblies, the House which draws its membership on the basis of the Population factor or index is regarded as the Lower House (and suffers all the implications of that categorisation) while the Upper House, the Senate, is that that draws its membership on the basis of the Equality of States principle. If we have a tri-cameral legislature at the world level, which draws its membership on the basis of the three factors of Population, Equality of States principle and Economic Power (read hi-tech and ability to produce the food, medicines and the other material innovations that help sustain life) which of the three Houses should be the Uppermost House? Of course, to my mind, there is no doubt that the House founded on the Economic Power index should take it. The Equality of states principle is about potentialities and probabilities, but the Economic power of a country is the reality on ground, a substantive thriving state of affairs! And this explains the veto status granted some of the technologically advanced nations at the

So, how do we reflect the above sentiment in a proposed World Legislature or a new United Nations? Perhaps we should have a tri-cameral Legislature at the world level after all, with the House founded on the basis of Economic Power playing the role of the Uppermost House in much the same way the Senate plays the role of Upper House in National Legislatures, producing the overall leader of the Legislature, notwithstanding the adjudged equality of both Houses in ordinary legislation.

VOTING POWER/SEATS FOR COUNTRIES IN EACH OF THE THREE HOUSES OF THE PROPOSED WORLD LEGISLATURE OR THE UNITED NATIONS

We now publish hereunder the projected voting powers/ Seats for all the countries of the world in each of the three Houses in a proposed Tri-cameral World Legislature beginning with the Uppermost House, with each House projected to have about 1,000 seats. Of course the Upper House (that based on Equality of States principle) will have equal number of seats for each of the 233 countries of the world. If we chose to make it 4 seats per country, then the House will be a (233 x 4) or 932-member legislative House.

THE UPPERMOST LEGISLATIVE HOUSE

Distribution of Seats for Countries in the Uppermost House of the Proposed World Assembly

Using the nominal GDP of nations, it can be shown that a total of 91 countries qualify to have seats in the Uppermost House of a future Tri-cameral World Legislature or Parliament with their respective number of seats as follows:

TABLE 7.1

Rank	Country	GDP (US$million)	% world GDP	No of Seats
	World [2019]	87,265,226		
1	United States	21,439,453	24.57	246
2	China	14,140,163	16.20	162
3	Japan	5,154,475	5.91	59
4	Germany	3,863,344	4.43	44

5	India	2,935,570	3.36	34
6	United Kingdom	2,743,586	3.14	31
7	France	2,707,074	3.10	31
8	Italy	1,988,636	2.28	23
9	Brazil	1,847,020	2.12	21
10	Canada	1,730,914	1.98	20
11	Russia	1,637,892	1.88	19
12	Korea, South	1,629,532	1.87	19
13	Spain	1,397,870	1.60	16
14	Australia	1,376,255	1.58	16
15	Mexico	1,274,175	1.46	15
16	Indonesia	1,111,713	1.27	13
17	Netherlands	902,355	1.03	10
18	Saudi Arabia	779,289	0.89	9
19	Turkey	743,708	0.85	9
20	Switzerland	715,360	0.82	8
—	Taiwan	586,104	0.67	7
21	Poland	565,854	0.65	7
22	Thailand	529,177	0.61	6
23	Sweden	528,929	0.61	6
24	Belgium	517,609	0.59	6
25	Iran	458,500	0.53	5
26	Austria	447,718	0.51	5
27	Nigeria	446,543	0.51	5
28	Argentina	445,469	0.51	5
29	U Arab E	405,771	0.47	5
30	Norway	417,627	0.48	5
31	Israel	387,717	0.44	4
—	Hong Kong	372,989	0.43	4
32	Ireland	384,940	0.44	4
33	Malaysia	365,303	0.42	4
34	Singapore	362,818	0.42	4
35	South Africa	358,839	0.41	4

36	Philippines	356,814	0.41	4
37	Denmark	347,176	0.40	4
38	Colombia	327,895	0.38	4
39	Bangladesh	317,465	0.36	4
40	Egypt	302,256	0.35	4
41	Chile	294,237	0.34	3
42	Pakistan	284,214	0.33	3
43	Finland	269,654	0.31	3
44	Vietnam	261,637	0.30	3
45	Czech Rep	246,953	0.28	3
46	Romania	243,698	0.28	3
47	Portugal	236,408	0.27	3
48	Peru	228,989	0.26	3
49	Iraq	224,462	0.26	3
50	Greece	214,012	0.25	3
51	New Zealand	204,671	0.24	2
52	Qatar	191,849	0.22	2
53	Algeria	172,781	0.20	2
54	Hungary	170,407	0.20	2
55	Kazakhstan	170,326	0.20	2
56	Ukraine	150,401	0.17	2
57	Kuwait	137,591	0.16	2
58	Morocco	119,040	0.14	1
59	Ecuador	107,914	0.12	1
60	Slovakia	106,552	0.12	1
—	Puerto Rico	99,913	0.12	1
61	Kenya	98,607	0.11	1
62	Angola	91,527	0.11	1
63	Ethiopia	91,166	0.10	1
64	Dominican Rep	89,475	0.10	1
65	Sri Lanka	86,566	0.10	1
66	Guatemala	81,318	0.09	1
67	Oman	76,609	0.09	1

68	Venezuela	70,140	0.08	1
69	Luxembourg	69,453	0.08	1
70	Panama	68,536	0.08	1
71	Ghana	67,077	0.08	1
72	Bulgaria	66,250	0.08	1
73	Myanmar	65,994	0.08	1
74	Tanzania	62,224	0.07	1
75	Belarus	62,572	0.07	1
76	Costa Rica	61,021	0.07	1
77	Croatia	60,702	0.07	1
78	Uzbekistan	60,490	0.07	1
79	Syria[n 4]	60,043/Na	0.07	1
80	Uruguay	59,918	0.07	1
81	Lebanon	58,565	0.07	1
—	Macau	55,136	0.06	1
82	Slovenia	54,154	0.06	1
83	Lithuania	53,641	0.06	1
84	Serbia	51,523	0.06	1
85	Congo, D Rep	48,994	0.06	1
86	Azerbaijan	47,171	0.05	1
87	Turkmenistan	46,674	0.05	1
88	Côte d'Ivoire	44,439	0.05	1
89	Jordan	44,172	0.05	1
90	Bolivia	42,401	0.05	1
91	Paraguay	40,714	0.05	1

971

NB: Calculated by the author with Data from the IMF

THE LOWER LEGISLATIVE HOUSE

Distribution of Seats for Countries in the Lower House of the Proposed World Assembly

Using the population of nations, it can be shown that a total of 133 countries qualify to have seats in the Lower House of a future Tri-cameral World Legislature or Parliament with their respective number of seats as follows:

TABLE 7.2

# Country	Pop (2019)	% World Pop	No. of Seats
World (2019)	7,713,468,100		
1 China	1,433,783,686	18.59 %	189
2 India	1,366,417,754	17.71 %	177
3 United States	329,064,917	4.27 %	43
4 Indonesia	270,625,568	3.51 %	35
5 Pakistan	216,565,318	2.81 %	28
6 Brazil	211,049,527	2.74 %	27
7 Nigeria	200,963,599	2.61 %	26
8 Bangladesh	163,046,161	2.11 %	21
9 Russia	145,872,256	1.89 %	20
10 Mexico	127,575,529	1.65 %	17
11 Japan	126,860,301	1.64 %	16
12 Ethiopia	112,078,730	1.45 %	15
13 Philippines	108,116,615	1.40 %	14
14 Egypt	100,388,073	1.30 %	13
15 Vietnam	96,462,106	1.25 %	13
16 DR Congo	86,790,567	1.13 %	11
17 Germany	83,517,045	1.08 %	11
18 Turkey	83,429,615	1.08 %	11
19 Iran	82,913,906	1.07 %	11
20 Thailand	69,625,582	0.90 %	9
21 U K	67,530,172	0.88 %	9

22 France	65,129,728	0.84 %	8
23 Italy	60,550,075	0.78 %	8
24 South Africa	58,558,270	0.76 %	8
25 Tanzania	58,005,463	0.75 %	8
26 Myanmar	54,045,420	0.70 %	7
27 Kenya	52,573,973	0.68 %	7
28 South Korea	51,225,308	0.66 %	7
29 Colombia	50,339,443	0.65 %	7
30 Spain	46,736,776	0.61 %	6
31 Argentina	44,780,677	0.58 %	6
32 Uganda	44,269,594	0.57 %	6
33 Ukraine	43,993,638	0.57 %	6
34 Algeria	43,053,054	0.56 %	6
35 Sudan	42,813,238	0.56 %	6
36 Iraq	39,309,783	0.51 %	5
37 Afghanistan	38,041,754	0.49 %	5
38 Poland	37,887,768	0.49 %	5
39 Canada	37,411,047	0.49 %	5
40 Morocco	36,471,769	0.47 %	5
41 Saudi Arabia	34,268,528	0.44 %	4
42 Uzbekistan	32,981,716	0.43 %	4
43 Peru	32,510,453	0.42 %	4
44 Malaysia	31,949,777	0.41 %	4
45 Angola	31,825,295	0.41 %	4
46 Ghana	30,417,856	0.39 %	4
47 Mozambique	30,366,036	0.39 %	4
48 Yemen	29,161,922	0.38 %	4
49 Nepal	28,608,710	0.37 %	4
50 Venezuela	28,515,829	0.37 %	4
51 Madagascar	26,969,307	0.35 %	4
52 Cameroon	25,876,380	0.34 %	3
53 Côte d'Ivoire	25,716,544	0.33 %	3
54 North Korea	25,666,161	0.33 %	3

55 Australia	25,203,198	0.33 %	3
56 Taiwan	23,773,876	0.31 %	3
57 Niger	23,310,715	0.30 %	3
58 Sri Lanka	21,323,733	0.28 %	3
59 Burkina Faso	20,321,378	0.26 %	3
60 Mali	19,658,031	0.25 %	3
61 Romania	19,364,557	0.25 %	3
62 Chile	18,952,038	0.25 %	3
63 Malawi	18,628,747	0.24 %	2
64 Kazakhstan	18,551,427	0.24 %	2
65 Zambia	17,861,030	0.23 %	2
66 Guatemala	17,581,472	0.23 %	2
67 Ecuador	17,373,662	0.23 %	2
68 Netherlands	17,097,130	0.22 %	2
69 Syria	17,070,135	0.22 %	2
70 Cambodia	16,486,542	0.21 %	2
71 Senegal	16,296,364	0.21 %	2
72 Chad	15,946,876	0.21 %	2
73 Somalia	15,442,905	0.20 %	2
74 Zimbabwe	14,645,468	0.19 %	2
75 Guinea	12,771,246	0.17 %	2
76 Rwanda	12,626,950	0.16 %	2
77 Benin	11,801,151	0.15 %	2
78 Tunisia	11,694,719	0.15 %	2
79 Belgium	11,539,328	0.15 %	2
80 Burundi	11,530,580	0.15 %	2
81 Bolivia	11,513,100	0.15 %	2
82 Cuba	11,333,483	0.15 %	2
83 Haiti	11,263,077	0.15 %	2
84 South Sudan	11,062,113	0.14 %	1
85 Dominican Rep	10,738,958	0.14 %	1
86 Czech Republic	10,689,209	0.14 %	1
87 Greece	10,473,455	0.14 %	1

88 Portugal	10,226,187	0.13 %	1
89 Jordan	10,101,694	0.13 %	1
90 Azerbaijan	10,047,718	0.13 %	1
91 Sweden	10,036,379	0.13 %	1
92 U A E	9,770,529	0.13 %	1
93 Honduras	9,746,117	0.13 %	1
94 Hungary	9,684,679	0.13 %	1
95 Belarus	9,452,411	0.12 %	1
96 Tajikistan	9,321,018	0.12 %	1
97 Austria	8,955,102	0.12 %	1
98 Papua New Guinea	8,776,109	0.11 %	1
99 Serbia	8,772,235	0.11 %	1
100 Switzerland	8,591,365	0.11 %	1
101 Israel	8,519,377	0.11 %	1
102 Togo	8,082,366	0.10 %	1
103 Sierra Leone	7,813,215	0.10 %	1
104 Hong Kong	7,436,154	0.10 %	1
105 Laos	7,169,455	0.09 %	1
106 Paraguay	7,044,636	0.09 %	1
107 Bulgaria	7,000,119	0.09 %	1
108 Lebanon	6,855,713	0.09 %	1
109 Libya	6,777,452	0.09 %	1
110 Nicaragua	6,545,502	0.08 %	1
111 El Salvador	6,453,553	0.08 %	1
112 Kyrgyzstan	6,415,850	0.08 %	1
113 Turkmenistan	5,942,089	0.08 %	1
114 Singapore	5,804,337	0.08 %	1
115 Denmark	5,771,876	0.07 %	1
116 Finland	5,532,156	0.07 %	1
117 Slovakia	5,457,013	0.07 %	1
118 Congo	5,380,508	0.07 %	1
119 Norway	5,378,857	0.07 %	1
120 Costa Rica	5,047,561	0.07 %	1

121 Palestine	4,981,420	0.06 %	1
122 Oman	4,974,986	0.06 %	1
123 Liberia	4,937,374	0.06 %	1
124 Ireland	4,882,495	0.06 %	1
125 New Zealand	4,783,063	0.06 %	1
126 C. African Rep	4,745,185	0.06 %	1
127 Mauritania	4,525,696	0.06 %	1
128 Panama	4,246,439	0.06 %	1
129 Kuwait	4,207,083	0.05 %	1
130 Croatia	4,130,304	0.05 %	1
131 Moldova	4,043,263	0.05 %	1
132 Georgia	3,996,765	0.05 %	1
133 Eritrea	3,497,117	0.05 %	1

1006

Calculated by the author using Population data from Worldometers (www.Worldometers.info) 2019. Elaboration of data by United Nations, Department of Economic and Social Affairs, Population Division.

WHAT THE PROPOSED WORLD ASSEMBLY IS NOT!

The proposed World Assembly is not by any stretch of the imagination to be likened to a world government. We make the distinction that just as it is wrong and futile to run a large heterogeneous country-state, like Nigeria, as a unitary state, instead of a federation that it should be, so will any attempt to run the world as a federation of states end up in chaos, ruins and regrets. The proposed World Assembly is therefore conceived to be a confederal organisation like the League of Nations and the United Nations before it that can only act on specific mandates given to it by nations of the world.

Like the United Nations, it is meant to take charge over a few matters of common concern to member countries – matters like world security, curtailment of environmental pollution, global warming, etc. But unlike the UN, distinction has to be made that the new organisation we propose must be inclusive. All the nations or countries of the world are to be part of the decision-making process of the organisation in line with democratic traditions.

Currently in the UN, it is only the few nations that are in the Security Council that are imbued with the power to take charge over the all-important security matters of the world while the vast majority of nations are side-lined and consigned to languish in the talk shop called the United Nations General Assembly, UNGA. The Security Council is not only there to make the rules but is also empowered to take direct action without reference or recourse to the UNGA.

Furthermore, the five permanent veto wielding members of the council are each empowered and entitled to veto any decision the council might make without minding where the rest of the members (permanent and non-permanent) stand. As a consequence of this provision, the Council is perpetually mired in grandstanding and stalemates thereby giving room for unhealthy and dangerous competition between especially the United States and Russia over which of them that becomes the world's policeman, with the EU, China, etc. waiting on the wings or playing a waiting game. The situation sustains the notion that world politics is a primitive politics system!

While this unhealthy competition is going on at all fronts, the international civil servants that man the executive arm of the UN dither, not wanting to be consumed by the rivalries among the big powers. The result is a mammoth weakening impact of the UN in its allotted area of responsibility and action. The situation is indeed most destabilising to the goals of the UNGA and the United Nations itself.

It is for the above reasons that we propose the tri-cameral Assembly that should remove a major problem that has for too long dogged and enfeebled the United Nations and in fact kept it from performing efficiently or excellently. It is our viewpoint that the veto must be abrogated. In its place each of the three Houses of the World Assembly is to establish its own house committee on security. And whatever decisions these committees reach in their respective domains are to be tabled for the ratification of each House, and these are to be harmonised in joint seating of the three houses in the usual legislative manner. The Assembly can then decide on sanctions or ostracism for erring member nations, and where necessary, practicable and plausible apply force by rallying member nations against a recalcitrant member. It is expected that the kind of support issues receive in the Assembly would go a long way in stimulating compliance by all and sundry.

Finally, we intimate that we are not particular about what name the Assembly should bear. If there is the will to restructure the UN to meet this proposal, then the name United Nations could be retained to carry on with the new mandate!

Achebe, Chinua, *Morning Yet on Creation Day*, London, Ibadan, etc. Heinemann, 1977.

Ajayi, J. F. Ade, *History of West Africa*, London, Longmans, 1971.

Amado, F. V. Garcia, *The Exploitation and Conservation of the Resources of the Sea. (A Study of Contemporary International Law)*, Leyden, Sijthoff, 1963.

Appadorai, A., *The Substance of Politics*. New Delhi, Oxford University Press, 11th Edition, 1975.

Aristotle, *Politics*. Translated by William Ellis. London, J. M. Dent (Everyman edition). 1912.

Billyou, De Forest, *Air Law*. New York, Ad Press, 1964. Birch, Anthony Harold, Representation. New York, Praeger, 1971.

Boguslavsky, B. M., et al, *ABC of Dialectical and Historical Materialism*. Moscow, Progress Publishers (English translation) 1978.

Brezhnev, Leonid I., *Reminiscences*. Translated from the Russian by Robert Daglish, Moscow: Progress Press, 1981.

- *Socialism, Democracy and Human Rights*, Oxford, Pergamon Press, 1980.

Broom, L. and Selznick, P., *Sociology*, New York, Harper & Row, 1963.

Brown, Norman O., *Life against Death*, New York, Random House, Modern Library Paperback, 1960.

Burgess, John W., *Political Science & Constitutional Law,* Boston, Gina, 1890 —91

Chase, James Hadley, *The Whiff of Money*, London, etc. Panther Book Ltd., 1970.

- *Tiger by the Tail*, London, etc. Panther Book Ltd., 1966. Center for International Studies Princeton University (ed. Sponsors).

World Politics (a quarterly journal of International Relations) Volume XVI, October 1963 — July 1964.

Chinoy, El, *Society; An Introduction to Sociology*, New York, Random House, 2nd Ed, 1967

Christenson, Reo M. (et al), *Ideologies and Modern Politics.* New York, Dodd, Mead, 2nd Edition, 1975

Cloward, Richard A. & Lloyd E. Ohlin, *Delinquency and Opportunity*, New York, Free Press, 1960

Cohen, Albert K., *Delinquent Boys*, New York, Free Press, 1955.

Cohen Maxwell (editor), *Law and Politics in Space*, Leicester University Press, 1964.

Dahrendorf, Ralf, *Class and Class Conflict in Industrial Society*, Stanford, Calif., Stanford University Press, 1959.

Dalen, Hendrik Van & Zeigler, L. Harman, *Introduction to Political Science*, Prentice-Hall, Inc. Englewood New Jersey 07632

Daniel, Wayne W. & James C. Terrell, *Business Statistics*, Boston, Houghton Mifflin Co. 2nd edition, 1979

Davidson, Basil & Buah, F.K, *The Growth of African Civilisation, (A history of West Africa 1000 — 1800)* London, Longman, 1965.

Demaris Ovid, *The Last Mafioso*, New York, Bantam Books, 1981

Dupuy, Rene-Jean, *The Law of the Sea (Current Problems),* Oceania Publications Inc. Dobbs Ferry N.Y., A. W. Sijthoff- Leiden, 1974.

Durbin, E. F. M., *Problems of Economic Planning*, London, Routledge and Kegan Paul, 1949.

Durkheim, Emile, *The Rules of Sociological Method*, Translated by Sarah A. Solovay & John H. Muller, Chicago, University of Chicago Press, 1938.

Eagleton, Clyde, *Responsibility of States in International Law*, New York, Kraus Reprint Co. 1928, Reprint 1970.

Ebenstein, W. & Edwin Fogelman, *Today's —Isms*, Prentice-Hall. Inc. Englewood Cliffs, New Jersey, 8th Edition, 1980.

English, M C., *An outline of Nigerian History*, London, Longmans, 3rd Impression, 1961.

Fage, J. D., *Introduction to History of West Africa*, London, Cambridge University Press, 3rd Edition, 1966.

Fawcett, James E. S., *International Law and the uses of Outer Space,* Manchester University Press, 1968.

Femi, Laura, *Mussolini*, The University of Chicago Press, 1961

Freud, Sigmund, *Civilization and its Discontents*, New York, Doubleday Anchor Books, 1958.

Goodrich, Leland M., *The United Nations in a Changing World*, Columbia University Press, New York & London, 1974

Gosch, Martin & Richard Hammer, *The Luciano Testament*, London, Pan Books/MacMillan, 1976.

Gotlieb, Allan, *Disarmament and International Law*, The Canadian Institute of International Affairs 1965.

Hitler, Adolf, *Mein Kampf*, with introduction by D. C. Watt, translated by Ralph Manheim, London, Hutchinson & Co.

La Palombara, Joseph G., *Politics within Nations*, Englewood translated by Ralph Manheim London, Hutchinson & Co., Cliffe, N.J. Prentice-Hall, 1974

Hook, Sidney, *The Hero in History*, London, Seeker & Warburg, 1945.

Hopkins, A. G., *An Economic History of West Africa*, London, Longman Group, 1973.

Isichei, Elizabeth, *A History of Nigeria*, New York, Longman, 1983.

Jarman, Thomas L., *The Rise and Fall of Nazi Germany*, London, The Cresset Press, 1955.

Jennings, Sir Ivor, *Party Politics II, (The Growth of Parties)*,

Cambridge, at the University Press, 1961.

- *Party Politics III, (The Stuff of Politics)* Cambridge, at the University Press, 1962.

Jhingan, M.L., *Micro-economic Theory*, New Delhi, Vikas Publishing House PVT Ltd. 1977.

Johnson, Harry H., *Sociology, A Systematic Introduction*, New York, Harcourt Brace & Co., 1960.

Johnston, Norman. et al (editors), *The Sociology of Punishment and Correction*, John Wiley and Sons, Inc. New York, 2nd Edition, 1970.

Kardiner, Abram, *The Individual and His Society*, New York, Columbia University Press, 1939.

Katz, Leonard, *Uncle Frank – The Biography of Frank Costello*, New York, Pocket Book ed., April 1975.

Kecskemeti, Paul, *Meaning, Communication and Value*, Chicago, University of Chicago Press, 1952.

La Palombara, Joseph G., *Politics within Nations*, Englewood Cliffe, N.J. Prentice-Hall, 1974

Laski, Harold Joseph, *The Grammar of Politics*, The Yale University Press, 1938

Lewis, John Royston, *Democracy; the Theory and Practice*, London, Allman, 1966.

Lipsey, Richard G., *An Introduction to Positive Economics*, E. L. B. S. & Weidenfeld and Nicolson,4th Edition, 1975.

Loveday, Robert, *Statistics — A First Course*, Cambridge University Press, 1958.

-    *Statistics — A Second Course*, Cambridge University Press, 2nd Edition 1969.

Macmillan, Harold, *The Middle Way*, New York, St. Martin's Press, 1966

Marcuse, Herbert, *Eros and Civilization*, Boston, the Beacon Press, 1955.

Marx Karl, *Capital III*, translated from the first German Edition by Ernest Untermann. Chicago, Kerr, 1909.

Marx, Karl & Friedrich Engels, *The Communist Manifesto*, Edited by D. Ryazanoff. New York, Russell & Russell, 1963.

Masters, Roger D, *World Politics as a Primitive Political System,* Published by Princeton University Press, 1964.

McKnight, Allan D., et al (editors), *Environmental Pollution Control, (Technical, Economic & Legal Aspects)*, London, Allen & Unwin, 1974.

McWhinney & Bradley, *The Freedom of the Air*, A. W. Sijthoff/Lyden, 1968.

M'Gonigle, R. M. & Zacher, M. W., *Pollution, Politics and International Law,* University of Columbia Press, 1979.

Miller, George A., *Psychology – The Science of Mental Life,* U. 8. A., Pelican Books, 1966.

Mills, C. Wright, The Sociological Imagination, New York, Oxford University Press, 1959.

Nixon, Richard, *The Real War*, London, Sidgwick & Jackson, 1981.

Nowak, Jolanta (editor), *Environmental Law – International and Comparative Aspects*, The British Institute of International and Comparative Law, 1976.

Oda, Shigeru, *International Control of Sea Resources*, A. W. Sythoff/Leyden, 1963.

\-   *The International Law of the Ocean Development: Basic Documents*, Lieden, Sijthoff, 1972.

Ogburn, William F., *Social Change*. New York, Huebsch, 1923.

Okigbo, P. N. C., et al, *Report of the Presidential Commission on Revenue Allocation (Federal Republic of Nigeria)* 1980.

Onwubiko, K. B. C., *History of West Africa. Book One: 1000 AD to 1800,* Africana Educational Publishers Co. Aba, Nigeria, 1967.

\-   *History of West Africa. Book Two: 1800 – Present Day*, Africana Educational Publishers, Onitsha, Nigeria, 1973.

Onwuejeogwu, M. Angulu, The Social Anthropology of Africa; - an Introduction, London, Heinemann, 1975. Parson, Talcott, *Theories of Society*, New York, Free Press, 1961.

Paxton, John, *World Legislatures*, London, The Macmillan Press Ltd., 1974.

Pentony, Devere E. (editor), *Soviet Behaviour in World Affairs: Communist Foreign Policies*, San Francisco, Chandler Publishing Co., 1962.

Pitkin, Hanna Fenichel, *The Concept of Representation*, Berkely, University of Calif. Press, 1967.

Plato, *The Republic*, translated by A. D. Lindsay. London, Melbourne, etc. S. M. Dent & Sons, 1976.

Redmond, P. W. D., *General Principles of English Law*, Plymouth, Macdonald & Evans, 1964.

Reijnen, Gibsbertha C. M., *Utilization of Outer Space and International Law*, Amsterdam, Elsevier, 1981.

Reisman, David et al, *The Lonely Crowd*, New Haven: Yale University Press, 1950, (Reprinted, Doubleday Anchor Books, 1953).

Russell, Bertrand, *History of Western Philosophy*, London, Unwin Paperbacks, 1979.

Sabine, George H. & Thomas L. Thorson, *A History of Political Theory*, Hinsdale Illinois, Dryden Press, 4th edition, 1973.

Schatz, Sayre P., *Nigerian Capitalism*, Berkely, University of California Press, 1978.

Schoehbaum, David, *Hitler's Social Revolution: Class and status in Nazi Germany 1933 —1939*, New York, Double day, 1966.

Sen, Chanakya, *Against the Cold War*, Bombay, Asia Publishing House, 1962.

Shinn, Robert A., *The International Politics of Marine Pollution Control*, New York, Praeger, 1974.

Shirer, William Lawrence, *The Rise and Fall of the Third*

Reich —A History of Nazi Germany, New York, Simon and Schuster, 1960.

Smith, Adam, *The Wealth of Nations, Vol. II*, edited by Edwin Cannan, Strand, Methuen & Co. Ltd., 1961.

Solzhenitsyn, Alexander, *The Gulag Archipelago 1.* Translated from the Russian by Thomas P. Whitney, Britain, Fontana, 6th Impression, 1979.

- *The Gulag Archipelago 3*, Translated from the Russian by H. T. Willetts, Britain, Fontana, 1978.

- The First Circle, Translated from the Russian by Michael Guybon, Britain, Fontana, 1970.

- *One Day in the Life of Ivan Denisovich*, Translated by Max Hayward and Ronald Hingley. New York, Bantam Books, 1963.

- *The Love-Girl and the Innocent*, Translated by Nicholas Bethell and David Burg. New York, Bantam Books, 1969.

Spiegel, Murray R., *Theory and Problems of Statistics, Schaum's Outline Series*, New York, etc., McGraw-Hill Book, Co., 1972.

Spufford, Peter, *Origins of the English Parliament*, London, Longmans, 1967.

Stride, G. T. & Caroline Ifeka, *Peoples and Empires of West Africa. (West Africa in History 1000 – 1800)*, Lagos, Nigeria, Thomas Nelson Ltd., 1971.

Tang, Peter, S. H., *Communist China Today*, Vol. 2. New York, Atlantic Book, 1958.

Teclaff, L. A. & Albert E. Utton (editors), *International Environmental Law*, New York, Praeger, 1974.

The Constitution of the Federal Republic of Nigeria, A Daily Times (Lagos) Publication, 1979.

Trevor-Roper, Hugh Redwald, *The Last Days of Hitler*, London. Macmillan, 1962.

Veblen, Thorstein, *The Theory of the Leisure Class*, New York, Random House, 1931.

Whittick, Arnold (editor), *Encyclopaedia of Urban Planning*, New York, etc., McGraw-Hill Book Co., 1974

Whyte, William H., *The Organisation Man*, New York, Simon and Schuster, 1956.

Wilson, Logan & William Kolb, *Sociological Analysis*, New York, Harcourt, Brace, 1949.

Wolin, S. & Slusser, R. M. (editors), *The Soviet Secret Police,* Connecticut, Greenwood Press, 1974.

Young, Roland, *Approaches to the Study of Politics, Evanston ILL.*, North-western University Press, 1958.

Young, Roland Arnold, *The British Parliament*, Evanston, North-western University Press, 1962.

1999 Constitution of the Federal Republic of Nigeria, Published by the Federal Government Press, Lagos, Nigeria.

INDEX

Adedeji, Prof Adebayo, 96, 99

African Development Bank (ADB), 124

Aristotle, 59, 102

Azikiwe, Dr Nnamdi, 117

Bakassi Peninsula, 85

Balzac, 13

Caesar, Julius, 101

Central Bank of Nigeria (CBN), 110

Concentration Camps, 15, 31

Cromwell, 4

Czechoslovakia, 19

Dictatorship of the Proletariat, 6, 7, 9, 11, 12

Economic determinism, 8, 9

Economic Policy Institute, 125, 126, 127, 130

Employee Compensation, 123, 152

Engels, Friedrich, 5

English Reform Act, 9

Federal Office of Statistics, 124

Friedman, Milton, 111

Galbraith, John Kenneth, 122, 125

Gestapo, 31

Glasnost, 21, 140

Gomulka, 19

Gorbachev, Mikhail, 21, 140

Great Depression of the 1930s, 11, 122, 123, 125

Hegel, 102

Heidensohn, 152

Heraclitian theory of constant flux, 102

Hitler, 34

Igbo Egalitarianism. 149

International Monetary Fund (IMF), 107, 108, 110, 111, 116, 180

Jacksonian revolution, 8, 9

James, William, 102

Karanzki, 21

Kerensky, Alexander, 10

Keynes, Lord, 112

Labour Party, 44, 45, 46

Laissez-faire, 37, 38, 39, 146

Lenin, Vladimir, 10, 11, 15, 16

Magna Carta, 4

Maoist era, 20

Mao-Tse-Tung, 22

Marahrens, Bishop of Hanover, 32

Marchais, 12

Marx, Karl, 4, 5, 6, 7, 8, 9, 10, 11 13, 57, 59

Masters, Roger D, 169

Mendelssohn, 33

Movement of individualism, 35, 83, 146, 147

Multi-party system, 53, 163

Mussolini, Benito, 25, 26

National Reich Church of German, 33

Nazi Party, 9

Neo-Keynesian remedies, 111

Nigerian Institute of Social and Economic Research (NISER), 123

Nixon, Richard, 29

Njoku, Charles, 99

Normal Distribution, 67, 70, 72, 73, 135, 149, 151, 158, 160

Nuremberg laws, 32

One Party System, 19, 53

Perestroika, 140

Peron, 31

Pinochet's Chile, 117

Solidarity Movement, 18, 19

Presidium of the Supreme Soviet, 20

Reich Food Estate, 34

Roosevelt, President, 145, 146

Roosevelt's New Deal, 145

Second World War, 31, 34

Shakespeare, 101

Shonekan, Chief Ernest, 99

Skewed Distribution, 67, 70

Social goods, 3, 58, 64, 66

Solzhenitsyn, Alexander, 15

Stalin, 11, 15, 16

Structural Adjustment Programme, SAP, 108, 109, 110

Surplus value, 5, 6, 13, 57

Totalitarian organisation, 26

Tri-cameral World Legislature, 177, 181

Trotsky, 11

Udoji Award, 123, 124

Underemployment Equilibrium, 112

United Nations (UN), 169, 176, 177, 185, 186, 187

Assembly United Nations General (UNGA), 169, 170, 175, 186, 187

Universal Suffrage, 12

Uppermost House, 176, 177

Vanguard of Communism, 11

Veto, 169, 186, 187

Veto Status, 172

Voting Power, 175, 177

Wage Growth in the US, 127

Wall Street crash of October 1929, 25

World Assembly, 170, 175, 177, 181, 185

World Bank, 107, 108, 110, 111, 116

World Legislature, 170, 175, 176, 177, 181

World Parliament, 177, 181

Worldometer, 185